DOG PROBLEMS

Carol Lea Benjamin

DOG PROBLEMS

A Professional Trainer's Guide to Preventing and Correcting: Aggression, Destructiveness, House-breaking Problems, Excessive Barking, Dogfights, Tugging, Jumping, Shyness, Stealing, Begging, Car Chasing, Fear Biting, Object Guarding, and much, much more.

Doubleday & Company, Inc., Garden City, New York
1981

Library of Congress Cataloging in Publication Data

Benjamin, Carol Lea.
  Dog problems.

  Includes index.
  1. Dogs—Training. I. Title.
SF431.B418   636.7'0887
ISBN: 0-385-15710-x
Library of Congress Catalog Card Number 80-1082

Portions of this book previously appeared in the magazine *Purebred Dogs/American Kennel Gazette.* © 1979, 1980 *Purebred Dogs/American Kennel Gazette.*

To Stephen J. Lennard, with love and admiration

The author wishes to express deep appreciation to:

Jim Menick and Nels Johnson at Doubleday
The American Kennel Club, the staff of *The Gazette* and especially
Pat Beresford, Editor-in-Chief, and Jan Saeger, Managing Editor
Robert Sherretta for advice and encouragement
Victoria Halboth for the out-of-sight recall and for cheerfully and
skillfully taking over all the work when I could not do it
Stephen Lennard for cutting, questioning and cheering on
Oliver Fox Benjamin, C.D., who is and always will be at the core of
my work with dogs

This book has been checked from the point of view of health and
safety by Dr. Alfred Grossman, Murray Hill Animal Hospital, New
York City.

CONTENTS

DOG PROBLEMS

Animals are such agreeable friends—they ask
no questions, they pass no criticisms.

—George Eliot, *Mr. Gilfil's Love-Story*

1

A Pound of Prevention

Never use a hatchet to remove a fly from the forehead of a friend.

—old Chinese proverb

Problem Prevention Through Understanding Your Dog's Nature

Human nature being what it is, and dogs being as clever as they are, it is fair to assume that, for as long as man has been dwelling with dogs, some dogs have discovered how to gain and keep the upper hand. This doesn't happen because they don't love us. It doesn't happen because they are, by nature, mean. It happens because, like wolves, they are pack animals, and it is an integral part of the nature of a pack animal to rise to the highest level he can.

A pack is a group of animals that live together, each dependent on the others for survival. In the wild, the pack provides protection, companionship, mates, baby-sitters for offspring, comrades for the hunt. There is a fierce loyalty within the pack and each member has a strong affection for the others. There is but one leader, usually a male, and until he is deposed by a stronger, smarter wolf, he calls the shots. Often the leader is the only male to mate. The female he chooses, the best around, will be the leader of the female subpack. He and she may mate for life.

This arrangement, made without any help from man, eliminates the possibility of overpopulation, of weak, sickly offspring, of starvation. Left to their own devices, the wolves maintain the balance of nature. Since usually only the "best" wolves breed, the health, strength and survival of the pack are well ensured.

Like his wild brother, the dog, too, is programmed for pack living. He must lead or be led. There is neither democracy nor anarchy in the canine world. A lone wolf cannot long survive; a dog without other dogs can, because he joins a family grouping of another species —a people pack. His dinner will be provided so that he needs no companions for the hunt. You will supply a mate if he is to have one and you will help care for the young. You will protect him when he is little and, in turn, he will protect you when he is grown. His affection will come from you. His love and loyalty will be yours in return. Who needs the wild?

On his own, he would not survive. He is no longer a creature of the wild. He has been domesticated—changed by selective breeding to suit the needs and desires of man. He will not be monogamous in his mating. The bitch will come into heat twice as often as her wild sister. No worries about overpopulation now. That's *our* headache. No longer will he be able to pick and choose his mate. No longer will he be free to roam and hunt. He's got roots now—and you may be more interested in tracing his than your own. His companionship, more often than not, will come from humans rather than from those of his own kind. While he craves and needs the company of other dogs, he will give his fiercest loyalty to a human being.

Some of his pack instincts, such as the protection of territory, will endear him to his new pack, thus ensuring his survival. Others, such as fighting over food, may sometimes cost him his life—that is, if the fight is with you or your children. His nature as a pack animal can be your biggest plus or his greatest minus. If leadership falls to him instead of you, you've got yourself a dog problem. If you take command, his penchant to follow a strong leader, an instinct which remains intact through domestication, can be the happy instrument by which you train him and take, once and for all, the upper hand.

Since your dog *must* have a leader, dear friend, you are elected—unless you want a dog to run the show at your house. It's really very simple. If he takes over, bullies you or bites you, he won't do it because he's perverted or disturbed, or because he doesn't love you. If he does it, he will do it because he is a pack animal with pack instincts. He will do it because he is a dog and something in him demands fulfillment of ancient programming. The drum beat he marches to has not changed much in thousands of years.

Since the dog is not built to live without a leader, what happens when this is the case? Being orderly by design, he seeks to end the chaos and anxiety caused by living in a manner incongruent with his nature—so he applies for the job himself. Making his stand with creatures of his own kind, he quickly finds out, with a growl, a push, a shove, a display of fangs and hackles, a strut on his toes, a step out of line, who the smartest, strongest dog really is.

Vying occasionally, even with you, for a higher position in the pack is part of the work of being a dog. Don't take it personally. When there's something important he wants to do, or when you've let your guard down for too long, or if you've set no limits or standards of behavior for him at all, he may try to juggle around the pecking order. More than likely, he'll do it without guns and tanks. His first display may be very subtle—a failure to come when called, a gentle nip, a small, almost inaudible rumble in his throat when you approach his dish, a sprinkle of urine on the side of your Bloomingdale's couch. If you let it go by, he'll continue. It's anyone's guess where it will end. That will depend on how assertive he is and how often you turn your back on his attempt to do anything he can get away with.

Long before tossing his hat in the ring, he'll have noted your strengths and weaknesses, your ability to be firm, your inconsistencies. In fact, shortly after joining your pack, your dog became the world's leading authority on you. His dependent position makes him observe you well. He's also well equipped to do so because he was raised in a different way than human beings.

Chances are, if you were raised like most people, your mother didn't break her neck to rush and comfort you every time you fussed or cried. You might have been fed on a schedule—and toilet-trained on one to boot. You don't have to read Freud to figure out that rigid schedules for input and output are not exactly in keeping with Mother Nature's design. Just examine the way the rest of her creatures mother their young.

When your puppy was little, his mom was never too busy boiling diapers to heed his cries. Besides, if she was a halfway decent bitch, she wasn't built to let him go hungry or unattended when he needed her loving touch. There was never a T.V. or a telephone to distract her. Her own mother had raised her in that same careful, sensitive way. No third party, right or wrong, ever gave her any instructions. She just did what came naturally—and what comes naturally is by definition always right.

As your puppy began to grow and develop, his mom did correct him sometimes with a nip, a slap or a shake for unacceptable behavior, but her anger was swift and her forgiveness swifter. She never made him go to bed without his supper. She never gave him the cold shoulder for the whole afternoon. What's more, she never made him feel guilty.

When we were little, things were probably a bit more complicated and the loving care we got was probably not so perfect. No puppy's mother ever overprotected or acted weepy and foolish if she didn't get a card on Mother's Day. No puppy's mother ever stopped her precious darling from doing things that just weren't her business because they didn't harm others or endanger him. A puppy grows up free to stuff himself when hungry, to relieve himself when he feels the urge and to explore his world, his littermates and himself. Restrictions were reasonable and continued to stand him in good stead even in adulthood.

While we were growing up, we learned that our desires would not always be fulfilled (even the very reasonable and urgent ones), that we should not only stop making mistakes, but should feel rotten about having made them in the first place, that our bodies and other people's were somewhat taboo—at least in places. As we learned to ignore many of our own feelings, we became unable to tune in to the feelings of others. Many of the restrictions placed on us, it turns out, are not to our advantage. To differing degrees, we got a little messed up and a lot out of touch. Anger was bad. Sex was dirty. Tears were unmanly.

Not so for puppy. Because your puppy was raised in a more natural fashion than you were, he remained more in touch. The world was less full of no-no's. He was able to retain the integrity of his own feelings and so be in touch with yours, too. Feelings of all kinds, yours and his, could resonate in his body. He grew up to doghood knowing when he was happy or scared or mad—and when you were.

Unblocked emotionally and unencumbered by language, your dog retained the ability to tune in to the reality of feelings—even hidden ones. Thus, he is intimately acquainted with the real you—a person you may not know very well yourself. In that sense, he reads the unconscious. The biggest mistake we make is to underestimate him. He, on the other hand, neither under- nor overestimates us. He reads us exactly as we are. So, if you think you're buying a watchdog and your German Shepherd ends up a lap dog, friend, you got what you wanted. Something in you broadcasted. Something in Killer received. Voilà! The lap Shepherd.

Vibes, ESP, call it what you will—this information is all around us, but we tend to ignore it. Fido, the clever little opportunist, tends to make use of it.

To be a good pack leader, you'll have to learn to read your dog, just as he reads you. Then you can use the information available to train him and understand him. It will help you to know when he's in trouble and when he's faking; when he's fighting mad and when he's just being a bully; when something is urgent or when he's merely giving it the old one-two. He'll know you know. A smart dog is smart enough to know when he can gain some ground. He's also smart enough to know, in short order, when he cannot. You'll be on top, and that's exactly where you belong.

Knowing his place, his limits, his leader, will give your dog a sense of order and security, but how can you communicate your status to him? You can do it his way—you can shove, bully, walk on your toes, you can raise your hackles, your eyebrows, your voice, a ruckus—or you can do it in a very simple, orderly, practical, human way. You can obedience-train your dog. The basic commands, available in many dog books or with the help of a professional dog trainer, will give you the basis of communication with your dog. He will learn first to focus his attention, then to listen to words, next to concentrate for longer and longer periods of time and, finally, to work. His attention will turn to you. He will understand rapidly that *you* call the shots and he will be more than just a happy dog. He will have the kind of language and manners that allow him to live well with humans, sharing space and pleasures, being neither a menace nor a pest. Training ensures your role as top dog and can be used periodically to remind him of that reality when he decides it's time to test you *again*. It is, therefore, the most essential element in dog problem prevention. It can make life with Fido a breeze. (Be sure to read Perfecting the Sit, Stay in Chapter 11 and Twenty-Five Tips for Better Dog Training in Chapter 16 for help in this area.)

Will he pine away for want of a role he cannot have? Will he hate the hand that trains him? No. He's not genetically programmed to grow bitter and spend his life on could-have-beens. The same clever architect who built us to act in the way we do, a way we refer to as human, built him to act the way he does, in a way we refer to as not human. He won't resent you for being in charge. In fact, the more confident and firm a top dog *you* become, the more secure he'll feel and the happier he'll be. Functioning within the limits you set for him gives him the anxiety-free life he needs. In gratitude and awe, he'll "dog" your footsteps and look upon your face with a devotion you'll never find in another human. That's not because we cannot love as well. The reason is that we are not pack animals and, despite the evidence of our history, we are not built to worship authority. Your dog is—so use this characteristic and enjoy it.

Now he's got a strong, benevolent leader. He's got a good home. He's trained so he has the run of the house and manners to go almost anywhere. You feed him, you brush him, you talk to him when you get home from work, you kiss his hairy head when so moved. What more could any dog ask?

Plenty.

Problem Prevention Through Constructive Use of His Mind and Body

Let's start at the top. He has a brain. You taught him SIT, DOWN, COME, STAY, HEEL, NO, OK, GOOD DOG, BAD DOG, DO YOU WANT TO GO OUT? and DID YOU DO THAT? Maybe you taught him GO PLAY IN THE OTHER ROOM, too. So he has a good beginning. But there are so many hours in the day. More than likely, you're away a lot—you're earning money, you're spending money, you're running, cycling or sitting in the movies, you're out with friends, you're visiting relatives, you're everywhere but home. Possibly your dog doesn't have another dog to play with—or even a cat. He doesn't care for soap operas, no one taught him to read, he can't knit. However, there is an energetic, functioning brain in his smart little head. If it doesn't get something constructive to do, well, you've been there, no?

Your dog's body is a marvelous piece of machinery, built to run and jump and swim and pull and leap and fight and take in nourishment and eliminate waste and sparkle and shine and be the center of attraction of any scene. It was not built to spend all day tied in the yard and all night in the garage. It is vital. It needs to be used. Your dog's mind and body both need exercise. Sometimes, they can be exercised right along with yours.

TEACHING YOUR DOG TO SWIM

Common sense and most state laws tell us that we shouldn't swim alone. Unfortunately, your dog does not qualify as another swimmer. Although some dogs have rescued drowning swimmers and will no doubt continue to do so, and Newfoundlands are being trained for water rescue work, *your* dog is more likely to get you *into* trouble in the water than *out* of it.

The problem is that most places that are safe for you are illegal for your dog. If there's a nearby swimming hole, duck pond, river or lake where *he* can wet his toes, *you* probably will have to stay dry—at least until he emerges from his swim and comes as close to you as possible before shaking.

If you are fortunate enough to have your own pool or lake or some other way of swimming with your dog, you've also got the best way to teach him to swim—by letting him follow you. He just won't want to stay on the shore when you start swimming away. So have another person around just in case you and your dog get cramps simultaneously, and don't let your dog swim right up to you, especially his first few times in the drink. Dogs have to learn how to swim properly. Until such time as they have taught themselves to swim smoothly, by trial and error, they are rather sloppy swimmers. They tend to swim almost upright and to thrash with their front paws. You can get an awfully bad set of scratches if you let your dog swim too close. A splash in his face may make him turn. If not, paddle and kick rapidly in another direction.

Swimming together can be wonderful, but your dog will get great benefits and great joy from swimming when you would rather curl up by the fireplace with a hot toddy. Many breeds and mixes love to swim year round, even in sub-freezing weather. This is fine unless you have a tiny Maltese or a thin-skinned Saluki. Retrievers, of course, were designed and built to swim in icy water and don't seem to notice the cold at all. It's best, in any case, if your dog is to swim in cold water, to keep him swimming all year round so that he gets used to frigid water temperatures gradually and is in shape for this more strenuous exercise.

Lots of dogs, after patient, initial introduction to the water, will retrieve a ball or stick until your arm is ready to fall off. It's one of the best exercises for most dogs—and most arms. Even if you are stuck waiting on the shore, you should get a lot of joy out of watching. Part of the fun of having a dog is the sheer expansiveness of observing him have a good time.

Caution should be exercised with heavy-coated dogs such as the Old English Sheepdog, the Komondor and the Puli. When they swim for long periods of time, their coats get heavy enough to cause them trouble; they could even drown. Usually a brief swim of fifteen or twenty minutes is safe and won't tire the dog so much that he is unable to carry the weight of his own wet coat. I'd also be careful with tiny, long-coated dogs; they could get tangled in shoreline plants and roots. When in doubt about your breed, check with your breeder.

For the dog who hasn't yet tried the water and won't follow you out, sometimes retrieving can be the winning ticket. One little Golden Retriever who was reluctant to do more than get her feet wet took off in a flash when one of the local regulars showed up to feed the ducks. She managed, on her first swim, to beat four mallards and two Canada geese to a large piece of bread. It seems she found eating and swimming easier than just plain swimming. Her subsequent dips were no problem at all.

No matter how you decide to tempt your Esther Williams into the water, never throw her in. She would swim. She wouldn't drown. But she may never want to do it again. In the long run, an *easy* first swim, accomplished by force, may be followed by a much longer dry period. It's better to proceed with patience than to scare the swimsuit off an innocent dog.

Swimming, while it ranks as one of the best and most injury-free exercises for both dogs and people, may cause your dog to have dry skin. This can easily be remedied. If your dog swims regularly, add some vegetable oil to his chow. Also, he'll be burning up a lot of

extra calories, so watch his waistline. If it's shrinking, add some
chow to his chow. Active dogs, like active people, can eat more food
and still stay trim. More's the fun.

EXERCISING? TAKE YOUR DOG ALONG

Whether you want to bicycle, run or roller-skate, your dog can get
in on the fun and the fitness. The principles of training are the
same; only the details will differ from sport to sport and dog to dog.

In order to run alongside your bike, your skates or your feet, your
dog must know how to heel reliably. Most dogs will automatically
move out to the left, leaving you a little more room to maneuver as
your pace picks up. If your dog is one of those who won't move over
as you speed up, hold your arm out to the left, leash in your left
hand, and tug him out in that direction as necessary. Do not increase your speed until he is running along smoothly at just the right
distance from you or your bike.

It is important to go slowly and cautiously while your dog is still a
novice jock. Before he's a seasoned athlete, he may bolt, trip you or
make unnecessary pit stops that could cause you a spill. If you do
get hurt, you'll never want to give him another chance. So while he's
a beginner, concentrate on him. It would even be a good idea to exercise without him and then take an extra run or spin around the
block just for the purpose of training him. Later on, when he knows
how to behave, he'll offer you a bonus of companionship and protection while you get in shape—and the exercise will be as beneficial
for him as it is for you.

You may notice an odd phenomenon when your dog begins to exercise with you on a regular basis. It's kind of like a runner's high,
canine style. After running along next to you for a few blocks, your
dog may get to a deeper level of concentration and look like he
could go on forever. He will run smoothly and will almost seem to
be in a rather pleasant semi-trance. Every dog I have ever run with
has appeared to go into this phase. All of them, in no time at all, became addicted to running.

If you're working out in a safe or protected area where your dog
won't interfere with others, where he can't get hurt by passing cars
and where there's no stringent leash law, you might let him run
along off-leash. Some leash laws, in fact, state that an off-leash dog
under control, with his owner present, is not inconsistent with the

law. So if your dog is trained well enough to plod along off-leash and, in case you need him, come quickly when called, you can let him choose his own pace and give him the joy of letting him run free. If you are running or cycling near a lake, he may even take a swim break and catch up to you later.

In a crowded area, near traffic or during prime time when everyone is out doing something, it is more considerate and saner to keep your dog leashed. Even dogs with flawless behavior can get into trouble in dense crowds.

Your dog should not exercise shortly after eating. Nor should he be given food or water, except for sips in hot weather, until a while after he stops panting. When your dog is exercising in hot weather, he should have water available all the time, except immediately after his run. He should be taken out early in the day or in the evening, rather than in the heat of the day. Since his cooling mechanisms are less efficient than ours, you should watch him to make sure he isn't too tired or too hot. When he is running in the heat, it is a good idea to wet him down, particularly his head, any time you pass a drinking fountain or open hydrant. In case of heat exhaustion or heat stroke, immerse the dog, except for his muzzle, in cool water if you can. Be sure to cool his head with water. Then get him right to your vet. With some commonsense care, you and your dog should both be able to exercise enjoyably and without mishap.

A well-exercised dog will not pace around indoors with ants in his pants. He will not be full of unused energy which could get used up in negative, destructive behavior. After his daily run, he'll be too tired to do anything but sleep.

KEEPING FIDO FED AND FIT

Improper diet can cause or add to dog problems, too. Again, common sense is your best ally. You don't need four years at Cornell Vet School to learn to read a dog-food bag. While there's controversy about exactly what dogs need in their diets, there's little controversy about what they don't need: sugar (which is used in large amounts to preserve the soft, moist foods), food coloring (which is used to please you, since your dog is color-blind) and preservatives (which are used to give the food a longer shelf life).

Just like you, your dog may get stuck with some things he doesn't need, even if you are a careful shopper. If dog food were made without preservatives and your dog's chow spoiled before you used it up, you might be an unhappy consumer. You may not be able to avoid preservatives in your dog's food, but you can avoid sugar and you can try for less food coloring. The best way to feed a dog is often a cheaper way, though not necessarily the cheap*est* way. The best way to feed a dog is really pretty easy, but not necessarily easi*est*.

Your dog has no need for food that looks like little hot dogs, little meatballs or little beef chunks—but isn't. He can't see that the "meat" is red. If he's anything like my dog, he probably wolfs his food down so fast he wouldn't know a crêpe from a blintze. He'll happily eat a good, plain, less costly diet of 80 percent dry dog chow and 20 percent supplement (cottage cheese, canned dog meat, plain yogurt, leftover vegetables, any whole-grain food, cooked eggs, liver, etc.). Your dog does not need (though *he* might disagree) ice cream, pizza, hot dogs, sugary cakes and cookies, croissants or pancakes with syrup. Sugar can make him hyper. So can additives. A plainer diet is better. He needs some fat added to keep his coat from getting dry—corn oil added to his dry chow will do. Some people like to add vitamins, too, for good measure—a multivitamin made for dogs, vitamin E for a shine on his coat, brewer's yeast to help keep fleas away. Variety is not essential. Sameness, oddly, is. The dog is a creature of habit. Familiar is good, so you can find a good food and stick to it. Just monitor the amount you feed—not by what the bag says, but by watching your dog's waistline. Next time you visit the supermarket, read those bags and cans. You only have to do it once.

Problem Prevention: The Good Life, Canine Style

Now that your dog has a degree in Fine Arts from Pratt, is eating at The Four Seasons and is pumping iron daily, can we stop worrying? Now have we prevented the possibility of dog problems?

Not entirely.

Many people want their dogs to jump out of the closet when they feel like having him show undying love and pant cutely for a few minutes—or they like the idea of a handsome, classy dog on a permanent DOWN, STAY in front of the fireplace. Not you. You know better.

The dog is a social animal. A social animal needs contact. Monkeys groom each other. Wolves work and play together. A dog likes to be with people. He needs to be touched. Petting makes him feel expansive—his muscles relax, his heart beats more slowly, his respiration becomes deeper and he feels terrific. He needs proximity. Just your presence is enough to make his tail wag. Doesn't that make you feel good?

Your dog doesn't need that much. He'd rather lie at your feet than in the basement. He'd rather go out with you than stay at home. He'd rather sleep on the floor near your bed than elsewhere in a bed of his own. He doesn't have to be on the couch, on your bed, on your lap—just around.

By giving your dog the good life—a little of this and a little of that—you move him further and further away from the thought, the notion, the possibility of becoming a problem dog. You'll have the lines of communication open. You'll know him better—body, mind and soul. You'll spot any symptoms of trouble much sooner than you would have before. You'll be his leader and your words will have clout. He'll be a happy dog. You'll be a happy master.

A dog is such a simple soul. He needs a few rules, some exercise and education, a balanced diet, a place to rest his weary head and the companionship of a loving master to make him feel secure and happy. These are the important ingredients for preventing dog problems. Your tone of voice, your posture, your attitude, your understanding will speak eloquently to him. Above all, remember his mother: be fair, be firm, correct him when necessary, forgive him rapidly and love him well.

Understanding what he needs and how he thinks will also help you to enjoy him even more than before—as a dog. Even if you put a coat on him, or little rain boots, he's still a dog. He's still nature's child, even groomed, clipped, polished and dressed. He still lives by his instincts, not by the book. He never reads an advice column to learn how to respond or react. Though his table manners are a scandal, though he'll mate or urinate in front of all your neighbors, he's exactly what we need in our plastic, mechanized, computerized, automated, space-age world. He's just a dog. He can show you a world of feelings in his soft, gentle eyes. He doesn't avert them when they are full of love. He is not ashamed. If we have lost Eden, he has not.

We may, as a people, have taken off a little weight and a little hair since those cave days so long ago. Our clothes have become more sophisticated, our table manners have improved, our dwellings have become permanent and some of us no longer throw rocks when we are angry or in love—but around the fire, begging for tidbits and bones, there's still a dog. Throughout the ages, he has endured. We still try to understand him so that we may better understand ourselves. Our canine connection goes deep to the core. It attaches us in some necessary and wonderful way to the earth from which we sprang, to which we belong and to which we shall surely someday return.

2

People and Dogs in Trouble

No one has yet programmed a computer to be of two minds about a hard problem, or to burst out laughing, but that may come.

—Lewis Thomas, *The Lives of a Cell*

Problem Solving and Assertiveness Training for Dog Owners

There are a variety of ways to attack a problem. Knowledge in the area of the problem is a strong, influencing factor. The better you understand the true nature of the problem, the more confident you will be. So the more you understand about the way dogs think and function, the more effective you will be in handling dog problems. It is, after all, easier to make a stand when you know the facts. However, when dealing with dogs, even after the facts are in, sometimes emotional aspects cloud our vision.

The person who coined the phrase "Love me, love my dog" was no dummy. Identification with our four-legged friends can run so deep and so strong that we lose the ability to see things as they are. If we can get over, once and for all, the idea that dog problems are equated with a lack of love from the dog to you, eyesight will improve rapidly.

There are several ways to face dog problems:

The Passive Method: "Maybe it will go away." Maybe it won't. "Maybe he'll outgrow it." Maybe he won't. Even if he will, it's a rather poor way to handle a dog problem. How many couches can you afford to lose waiting for him to outgrow the chewing stage? Some dogs, left uncorrected, chew their way from birth to senility, but any dog can learn to be happy chewing a bone once he learns the no-no's from the yes-yeses.

Passivity, just waiting, looks like the easy way. Often, it's the expensive way. Training can rush nature. Prevention can save your household goods. Why just turn your back and grit your teeth when other methods are available.

Dog problems do not remain static. Sometimes they *do* go away by themselves. Usually, they get worse. If they are part of your animal's pattern of testing and your response is passive, they will definitely get worse. There is a method to his madness. While you may not have understood why, after all these years of being housebroken, he suddenly jumped up on your bed and urinated, perhaps you can understand now. Some assertive fellows try to bite the hand that feeds them when they are still sporting diapers. Other dogs ripen late in life. They mature slowly and their languid body development is matched by what is not exactly the fastest brain in the West. It may not even occur to them, until three or four years of age, that maybe, just maybe, your pack could be theirs for the taking—or even the asking. Voilà! Urine on the bed. A passive response? Not from you.

The Active Method: Some owners, with or without much understanding of the nature of dogs, meet problems head on. Their common sense, their sense of dignity, their ability to mobilize justifiable anger, all reach the same conclusion: "Not on *my* bed you don't!" Bravo for them.

They may go too far. They may yell too loud. They may hit when unnecessary. They may need improvement. Basically, though, they are on the right track. In a sense, who *cares* why your dog marks your bed? He just *can't.*

People who handle problems assertively experiment until they find a correction that the dog hates enough to stop him from doing whatever he is doing that his owner hates. This, classically, is the basis for most dog training. If we stopped here, it wouldn't be terrible. But we don't have to stop here. For most problems, better methods—more exciting and productive solutions—do exist. Too much of hitting the nail on the head can be a bad thing. This is especially so if the nail is your dog. Sometimes, an acceptable method, overused, can cause problems itself. So if every time your dog blinks sideways he gets it in the chops, you may be stopping him from urinating in the house only to find that, in self-defense, he becomes a biter or that you've made him a nervous wreck.

Handling problems assertively and directly can be fine, but communication is the key. Does your dog know why he is being corrected? More important, what is happening to the energy and drive that was going into the problem? Aside from the problem of overkill with this method, we are also dealing with leftover energy. Hence, the next step.

The Serendipitous Method: This new way to train dogs was thus named because I discovered it, quite by chance, while observing dogs I was training. While trying to find new and better ways to solve both common and unique dog problems, it occurred to me that if the dog's energy could be rerouted, things would go rapidly and smoothly. This method of handling dog problems is faster, easier and more effective than previous methods. Furthermore, it leaves the dog not only problem-free, but smarter and more fun to be around.

The Serendipitous Method leaves nothing hanging. Instead of merely stopping an activity, when this method is applicable you will redirect the activity. "No, you can't pull and tug on my kids' clothes, but you can do it on this knotted rope. You can have all the pulling and tugging fun you want, under my direction and my control." A terrific boon to dogs and owners, this method allows the dog to play out some of his needs without being pesty, dangerous or destructive.

There's a force of energy and intelligence operating behind any activity. You may not think it intelligent for your dog to chase your children and their friends, nipping at their heels, but he is actually using his herding instinct. Is it his fault that, generation after generation, his genes were carefully selected to strengthen this instinct? Is it his fault that you fell in love with the cute, shaggy face of a Bearded Collie, a dog valued for his ability to turn in a good day's work and to work, like most sheepdogs, with little direction from man? Can you blame him, or any dog, for playing out his heritage? If you don't give your Beardie or Komondor or Puli a good day's work, if you haven't provided sheep or cattle for him to be responsible for, for him to move hither and yon, is it any wonder that he sees your little herd as his own?

Sure, you can belt him in the chops when he chases your kids. Sure, you can stop him. Certainly, you can't keep a herd of sheep in your four-room apartment—but what is your dog supposed to do when he hears, loud and clear, the music of a shepherd boy's horn wafting toward him? What have you provided to use up that energy, to exercise his herding "smarts"? He was bred and born to work. The unemployed always have problems.

By use of the Serendipitous Method, you can help your dog use his drives and instincts and energies constructively instead of destructively. Instead of merely turning away the flow of energy from his desired direction, you will direct where it goes. You will take this opportunity to create better rapport with him, to exercise your own inventiveness and to take one small step toward the end of dog problems.

Begin to observe your dog and see what he is actually *doing*. Don't concentrate only on problem behavior—check out all his activities. Start putting two and two together. Several different activities may be the result of one frustrated drive. If he nips at passing feet, if he chases cars, if he's fascinated by anything moving across the floor, if he attacks your vacuum cleaner, if he sleeps across the doorway to your children's room, he may have a very strong, very thwarted instinct to herd. Now you can begin to name replacement activities.

By interfering with any activity, you have already begun to take control. *Just by naming an activity, before redirecting it, it begins to belong to you.*

Sometimes, as with tugging, you can name and encourage exactly what your dog is doing and enjoying. All you want to do is take control so that you can change the object being tugged. You can teach your dog to tug a dog toy or a rubber figure eight instead of your kids' pants. Sometimes, you must deal with the *spirit* of the activity. A herding animal needs to run and chase. Tell him CATCH ME,

CATCH ME and play tag with him. Controlled tag is not the same as his former herding of the kids. Any activity *you* name and encourage, you will also be able to stop on command. Your little sheepherder was also bred to feel responsible. You can give him jobs to do around the house—collecting socks from the floor if he likes to retrieve, barking at the door when the bell rings, fetching the newspaper. Obedience work will give him responsibilities. For a house pet, training also fulfills the dog's strong need to work. Your dog can enjoy changing the object of his activity or replacing one kind of work with another. He's flexible.

When the energy involved in a problem activity is used up in another way, you have both prevented and corrected the problem. Keeping this in mind, we will use the Serendipitous Method whenever possible, sometimes in combination with one or two other methods. We're flexible. The goal is a satisfied, healthy, happy, problem-free dog and a happy, almost smug, dog owner. Problems will be dealt with individually in the chapters to follow.

How To Learn by Looking at Your Dog

Before you begin to deal with your own dog's problems, it is important to assess the dog carefully. You cannot hope to solve a problem if you don't understand it well, if you don't know exactly what it is. You can pinpoint and clarify each problem by observing your dog in a new way before you begin to retrain him.

All too often, I have seen well-meaning trainers rush in on dogs, grabbing the leash, setting the pace, demanding and getting instant obedience. I have, out of anxiety and a need to prove myself capable, done so myself. Poor dogs. This is no way to learn.

Although I have been assisted in my education by many along the way—trainers, fanciers, handlers, owners, groomers, books, films, overheard conversations (I'll take my education wherever I can get it)—my best teachers have been the dogs themselves. I no longer rush. I wait and *see*. When there's a problem, I look at the dog for the answer. You can learn a lot by looking.

Generalizations are an important beginning. It is necessary to know about dog behavior, about the behavior of your dog's breed, about the behavior and temperament of the line from which your dog emerged, about his sire, his dam, his littermates. But the most significant information comes only from your dog. When there is no

other information, when you cannot understand him in the context
of his relatives, he is available, a walking history—if only you will
look. The information which comes from *him* is the only information you can be sure applies to *him*. So begin to observe him growing, changing, full of surprises—not just during puppyhood, but as
long as he is alive.

THINGS TO OBSERVE

His Timetable: Does your dog bound into your room at the crack
of dawn, raring to go, hopping to get out, alive, awake, full of energy
—or does he get up slowly at the crack of noon and need two cups
of coffee to get his eyes open? Is his peak period of activity early in
the day or late? Does he get peppy or sleepy after his meal? Is he
more lethargic in hot weather? Does he hate the rain or the cold?
You ought to know. You ought to work him when he's full of
energy—and work him well enough so that he will work for you at
bad hours and on off days, if he has to. However, if you know him
well, you can also let him lie in front of a fan with a tall something
to drink on hot days when he's too pooped to move. Watch him.

His Style—With People: Is he a wise guy, forever testing? Is he
overly submissive? Does he push you, ever so slightly, when you are
out for a stroll? Do you find yourself walking more and more to the
right when he is at your left side? If so, he may be working his way
to the top. Push back, ever so slightly—and ever so clearly. Some
dogs take the submissive route to the top. They put on a big show—
ears back, leg up, roll over and show the belly, stain the carpet just a
tad—and all to get you not to punish them. Then, behind your back
or right in front of your face, they do as they please. Please note.
Does your dog act assertive with women and submissive with men?
Is he just an easygoing slob, happy to obey any command? Is he
aloof—neither pushy nor submissive, just cool? Knowing these
things will help you understand him and train him properly.

His Style—With Dogs: Contrary to what I have read, I have seen
that the way a dog behaves with dogs is not necessarily a reflection
of the way he will behave with people. He may be macho with other
males and pushy with females and yet be obedient and tractable
with humans.

Still, it is well to note how your dog behaves with other dogs and to retain this information along with all the other facts you discover about him. Sometimes what you see will require some action on your part. A female, for example, who is always submissive to other females, even those younger than she, may lack confidence so badly that she takes the path of least resistance in all situations. Just to make sure, she plays dead. This may make her less acceptable as a pet or as a show dog. Confidence building can be done through gradual exposure and obedience work done with a light, firm hand and much praise. Your progress can be tested by observation.

The Eyes Have It: Last—and first—when you want to know who lies behind the fur mask, look at your dog's eyes. They are, as the saying goes, the mirror of the soul. Many say that direct eye contact may be viewed as aggression by the dog. While this is certainly true in the wild, where only the alpha wolf makes direct eye contact, it is not true across the board. Pet dogs learn to make soft and loving eye contact from their human pack leaders. They learn to *see* more like humans and less like wolves when they are dealing with humans. You can even observe this exciting part of their education happen next time you have a litter or raise a puppy. You may find that your little puppy will not make eye contact or that if he does he will not hold it for very long. He'll glance at your eyes and then quickly avert his. Gradually, as you look at him lovingly, he will be able to return that look to you.

Other than in situations where the threat or possibility of aggression is strong, eye contact with dogs is usually safe and profitable. If you look into your dog's eyes, you will see a lot of what he is made of—his seriousness, his sense of humor, his feelings of affection, all his real feelings. You will see when he's sad, angry or scared and, very often, when he is in need and what he is in need of.

Looking at dogs is a party for the eyes. Watching them move with natural grace and energy and joy is an expansive experience. Furthermore, the amount of information to be picked up free for the looking is worth its weight in dog books. So, before you train, take a good look at your best friend for the pure pleasure and the rich educational experience it will give you. Now you are ready to get to work.

3

Housebreaking

Neatness counts.

—Everybody's third grade teacher

A housebreaking problem should be readily definable and, pardon the pun, easy to spot. However, many people think they have housebroken dogs who just have accidents once in a while. I have heard reports of the once in a while being as often as several times a day!

If your young dog loses a few drops of urine when he greets you, particularly if he takes on any other aspect of submissive behavior such as lifting a paw, lifting a hind leg, rolling over or exposing his belly, this is not a housebreaking problem. It will, however, be covered in this section so that you know how to avoid making it a housebreaking problem.

If your dog of any age is ill or on medication and he has an accident, this is not a housebreaking problem. Your dog will probably be so mortified that you will find it hard to behave as a proper pack leader. Therefore, this problem will be covered in this section, too.

If, for any other reason—rain, snow, sleet, dark of night, it's Tuesday, it's not Tuesday, or the classic "I forgot!"—your dog urinates or defecates in your house, your dog is not housebroken. If he's a puppy, he's just not housebroken. If he's over six or seven months old, you've got a housebreaking problem.

Preparing Puppies for Rapid, Easy Housebreaking

Dogs are creatures of habit. Whatever world you show them, that's the world they'll believe in. As newborns, they need the stimulation of their mother's licking to help them to eliminate wastes. In that way, the den is kept clean and the puppies thrive. When they are still tiny, still blind and deaf, the stimulation of eating begins to work wonders on its own. Still, their devoted mother ingests all their wastes and keeps the den tidy.

Some mothers, as well you know, are better than others. I'd be willing to bet that the more scrupulously clean the mother keeps the den, the easier it is to housebreak those puppies. Believing that, when my own stalwart little bitch Fanny had her first litter, we lined the whelping box with newspaper; my daughter and I changed it as often as our energies would allow—at least five times a day. In between, Fanny did her job. Our eight puppies got so used to being clean and dry that when one of them stepped into a wet spot (they still could not see) it would shake its foot and cry. They just didn't like walking around in urine, and who could blame them?

Poor initial upbringing has been the downfall of many a puppy as well as many a person. When you buy a puppy someone else has whelped and raised, what has happened before you came into his life may have taught him to be dirty or just not to give a hoot. Fall asleep in his cereal? Sure—and in anything else that's around, too.

Some owners add to this bad early training without meaning to. They leave the puppy in a room with papers for him to soil. Often, particularly if it's an isolated area of the house, such as the laundry room or someplace in the basement, they are not too regular in cleaning up. The message as your dog reads it is that it's okay to soil in the house. If it weren't, why would you leave the mess there?

The best thing you can do for your puppy and yourself is to clean up quickly. In this way, your message is loud and clear—or perhaps I should say "Loud and clean." Time and time again I have been called in on a housebreaking consultation where a big part of the problem had to do with negative subliminal messages. But whatever happened before did not ruin your dog. He's well equipped to relearn. So if you mind a dirty floor, make sure he does, too. Clean up now—not later. Wash the area, every time, with a cleaner containing ammonia. If the accident is on your rug, clean the spot and then dab it with white vinegar instead of ammonia, which could stain. The ammonia or the vinegar will neutralize the odor that inspires your dog to keep returning to the scene of his crime.

Cleanliness is only one of the ways you'll get through to your dog without yelling, hitting or threatening to call the pound. Remember, we are dealing with a den animal. His survival depends upon a clean nest. So if we simulate the den by placing the puppy in a very small area, he will, by relying on nothing but his own instincts and without much work on your part, begin rapidly to learn how to pace his need to eliminate so as to stay clean between outings. Most animals have a natural desire to keep the area where they eat and sleep clean. We can capitalize on this convenient fact of life to communicate to the dog and get a necessary job done quite easily. If the dog you are trying to housebreak seems to be a dirty one, it is very possible that somewhere along the line he was taught to be that way. A pet dog cannot control his own environment. He has very little choice. Left alone in a dirty pen with his littermates or in an uncleaned playpen or other small area by himself, the puppy is unable to get a mop and bucket and clean up. He simply adjusts.

Housebreaking With a Crate

Housebreaking a puppy or a grown dog with the use of a wire housebreaking crate simply means formalizing the information above into a housebreaking regimen. You know your puppy would prefer to stay in a clean, dry area if given the chance. You know he is built to keep his little den clean. So a schedule has to be formulated, humane to him and possible for you. He will get used to going out on that schedule, on time, *please*, and staying in his clean, dry, small den—the crate—in between. At least, that's what he'll do until he's housebroken. Once he catches on, he'll need a little bit of time until this habit is established. Then he'll get progressively longer and longer periods of freedom after each walk and before he is again confined in the crate. Eventually, he will be reliable enough to have run of the house. Easy? You bet.

First, let's talk about the crate. No, it is not cruel. Providing a den for a den animal is not cruel. Although it may look like jail, since it is made out of wire, it isn't. The fact that the crate is wire allows cool breezes to blow over your hot dog's body and allows him to see what's going on around him when he's inclined to look. The crate, often made so that it is collapsible, will also be a handy piece of equipment for other problem correction and prevention. It is also the best and safest way to take your dog traveling. Crated, he will be unable to jump out of the car and get lost or hurt. He'll feel secure. You'll be able to save money on boarding by taking him with you on vacations. Motels and even hotels often accept dogs in the rooms if you have a crate. It assures the management that your dog will not eat their beds, rugs and walls. Even reluctant relatives may invite you with canine when they know he can be crated when no one's watching him. Besides, all kinds of messages are getting through to him as he learns to accept the confinement of the crate—messages that will help you to train him and stay in charge.

For housebreaking purposes, the crate should be the size of the puppy. If it is larger than his reclining body, he can go to one end and eliminate and go to the other end and lie down. Since one end is pretty close to the other, he'll end up walking and sleeping in urine and feces—the exact opposite of what we are after. The extra space would also enable him to move about. Moving about would make him need to eliminate. So the small-size crate both encourages cleanliness and minimizes the need to evacuate. Naturally, the crate is being used as a teaching tool and the puppy will be given as much freedom as he can handle all throughout the housebreaking period. He just should not have enough freedom, in or out of the crate, to allow him to have accidents indoors.

If you'd like to double and triple the mileage you get for your money, and who wouldn't, buy a crate that will fit your dog's adult size and, for housebreaking, make it smaller with a piece of wood or a wire rack. Once your dog has the idea, anyway, the bigger size will do just as well.

Many people ask if they can put something on the bottom of the crate so that the dog will not have to lie on the cold metal surface. Many dogs prefer the cold surface. However, you can put anything you like in the crate as long as your puppy doesn't take that thing as an invitation to eliminate. If you have already paper trained the puppy, it would not be a good idea to put paper in the crate. A towel may make your puppy feel cozier, but he might urinate on it. Since the towel will absorb the urine, it won't run all over the crate. The puppy can then bunch it into a corner and stay dry. In that way, the towel might allow the puppy to cheat. Of course, that won't help his training any. Some puppies will make a chew toy out of a towel or anything else you put in the crate. If it makes you feel better, try one old towel. If your puppy wets it or tears it, remove it and let the puppy stay in the empty crate.

The next question is whether or not anything can go into the crate to feed or entertain the puppy. The whole idea of the crate is to imitate a natural environment that will encourage the puppy to quickly and easily teach himself to eliminate out of doors on a schedule suitable to his needs and your time restrictions. The idea is not to torture him, bore him, make him miserable. Of course, he can have a ball or a bone to chew. You may, if you think it will entertain him, leave a radio playing and hope that the music will soothe his savage breast. Food, on the other hand, is not a terrific idea, since it will give him a need to go out. That may happen when you are away at work.

His eating habits naturally will be another factor in the housebreaking process. It is a mistake, in an attempt to be kind, to leave food available for long periods of time or even all day long. All other factors aside, this is a very poor way to housebreak a dog. Constant eating means constant elimination. Puppies should be fed on schedule, depending on when you can whisk them out of the crate and out of the house. Food should be left down for no more than fifteen minutes. Dawdling over food is a bad habit. It may also encourage two other bad habits—his of not being housebroken and yours of cooking little specialty items because he's acting fussy about his dog food. Veal scallopini is far too expensive. Let him stick to dog food and fifteen minutes. Losing a meal once or twice for acting slow and picky will encourage him to chow down efficiently when it's mealtime. So much for veal scallopini.

Unless the weather is ghastly and you have no air conditioning, you will not have to leave water in the crate. If you did, it would create the need to urinate—possibly off schedule, since the puppy is young. However, the puppy should have as much water as he likes when he is out of the crate. Once he is housebroken, he should always have an ample supply of fresh water. Water is essential for his health—for digestion, for safe excretion of chemical wastes from his kidneys, for his body's ability to cool itself. Deprivation of water would be harmful.

If you are worried about leaving no water in the crate while you are out to work, leave a couple of ice cubes to melt in a dish. In this

way your puppy can wet his whistle without ingesting huge amounts
of liquid. Also, the water available as the cubes melt will last longer
than a bowl of water.

Our next job is the preparation of a schedule. I would no more
ask you to get up at an ungodly hour than I would ask your young
dog to wait more than a maximum of eight hours before going out,
so some compromises are in order. If you must have lights out by
eleven, your puppy must be up and out of doors by seven. Cheer up.
When he's an adult, he can and will wait longer overnight. But
while he's young and learning, eight hours is really all he can wait.

Here is a sample walking and feeding schedule which you can
amend for your hours, keeping in mind that you can only get an
extra hour's sleep in the morning by staying up an hour later in the
evening. No cheating.

PUPPY SCHEDULES FOR HOUSEBREAKING

If you are at home		*If you work all day*	
A.M.		A.M.	
7:00	Walk	7:00	Feed; Walk
7:30	Feed		Play in kitchen while you eat breakfast
7:45	Walk	8:00	(or just before you leave) Walk
	Fifteen minutes play in kitchen		Confine in crate
	Confine in crate		
P.M.		P.M.	
12:00	Walk	6:00	Walk
	Fifteen minutes play in kitchen	6:20	Feed
	Confine in crate	6:40	Walk
4:00	Feed; Walk		Twenty minutes play in kitchen
	Fifteen minutes play in kitchen	7:00	Walk
	Confine in crate		Confine in crate
7:00	Walk	11:00	Walk
	Fifteen minutes play in kitchen		Confine overnight
	Confine in crate		
11:00	Walk		
	Confine overnight		

The stay-at-home schedule, naturally, is easier on your puppy—but if you have to work, you have to work. People do not tend to quit their jobs when it's time to housebreak a dog. However, if there's a nice kid or friendly neighbor who can get in and walk the puppy once in the middle of the time you are out, it would be terrific. If there's no possibility of that, the puppy will have to adjust.

Only you will know your own puppy intimately. Therefore, only you can adjust the schedule realistically. Fifteen or twenty minutes of play in the kitchen (not on the rugs) is what the average puppy can do before needing another outing. But here, above all, common sense should prevail. Suppose the kids want to play with the puppy and it's in between walks. You can say "No" to the kids. Or you can say "Yes" and have them walk the puppy before they play with him. In fact, they can just play with the puppy outside. There's no harm in that. Any time you or they have the time or the desire to play with the puppy out of doors, do so. If the puppy wets when outside, that's just fine. If you praise him every time he does, you'll speed up housebreaking by motivating him.

Your puppy may stay dry for only five minutes—or for an hour. If so, change the schedule so that it's right for *him*. Walk him. Praise him warmly for evacuating in the great outdoors. Bring him in and play with him or just let him romp in the kitchen while you prepare a meal or have a coffee break. Then, with the company of his favorite toy, crate him until the next outing. Most puppies will make excellent use of their crate time by catching up on lost sleep and growing.

If the puppy soils your kitchen, he's been out of the crate too long —or he didn't do what he was supposed to do outside. Where else could he do it, in that case, but inside? If the walk was a dud, put the puppy right back in the crate until his next scheduled walk. This is how you can communicate to him what this whole experience is all about. If the puppy soils the crate, it's either because it's the first or second time he's in it, and he doesn't know yet that he'll be stuck with it for a while, or the crate is too big. When he does have an accident in the crate, scold him, walk him, praise him if he goes outside and *clean the crate*. Remember, we want him to loathe being dirty. So never intentionally leave the puppy in the soiled crate or put him back in a dirty crate after an outing.

Now the puppy is getting into the swing of things. He does indeed empty himself when out on walks. He keeps the crate and

kitchen dry. Now you can begin to expand the time he is out playing, moment by moment. Do not rush. In the case of housebreaking,
faster is often slower in the long run. If he's fine for a week, give
him twenty minutes of play after his walk the next week and maybe
thirty minutes at a time the week after that. After a few months,
he'll be able to play in the kitchen for an hour or two at a time.
Now you can begin to leave him alone in the kitchen. You can also
start to experiment with tiny doses of freedom in other rooms. Prior
to this time, he was never in the position to have an accident unnoticed. Now you can take him exploring in the rest of the house and
begin to give him freedom, five or ten minutes of it at a time, in
rooms other than the kitchen, both monitored by you and alone.

If he backslides, even once, he goes back to the first week's schedule for a full week. Then you'll creep slowly toward giving him the
run of the house again, one small step at a time. Expect him to
backslide a few times. No owner could be so lucky as to have a dog
who never lost his head on the pale blue oriental rug. Life just
doesn't work that way. So do not feel frustrated if your housebreaking dance goes forward and backward. The job *is* getting done.
Dogs learn a lot from their mistakes.

Confinement Without a Crate

This same principle can be employed even if you can't get or
don't want to buy a crate. However, I strongly urge you to make the
purchase, since the crate can and will be used for many other things.
It is far and away the best method for housebreaking dogs of any
age.

If you do not have a crate, you can block off an area that will be
the size of a proper crate and use this area for confining the dog.
Some dogs will keep a larger area, such as a bathroom, clean. You
can experiment as long as you don't stick to an area whether it
works or not. If the kitchen works as a crate and your dog keeps it
clean, that's all well and good. If he wets in a corner of it, even
twice a week, the job's just not getting done. If you go on thinking
that it is, you'll just be fooling yourself. The right size den—and this
will vary from dog to dog—will keep your dog as dry as a bone.
That, and only that, is the aim of this game.

Correction and Praise

Communication being the goal, we have to let pooch know that when he squats on the grass we're happy and when he does it on the kitchen floor, we're not. Now hear this! Forget everything you heard elsewhere. *Do not hit your dog with a rolled-up newspaper.* Do not, in fact, hit your dog with anything. Hitting is totally unnecessary at this point and should remain so.

When your dog eliminates where you want him to, pat his head and warmly tell him he's a good boy. That's it. Do not jump up and down. Do not talk in a high-pitched baby voice. Do not offer him treats. All that hysteria plus the presence of food will make him instantly forget what you're so happy about. Be calm. Housebreaking, when you think about it, is just a normal part of having a dog. It's no big deal.

When your dog goofs, on his way out for a walk or during an illicit raid through the house when he gets away from you, do not call him to come and then punish him. If you do that, he'll stop coming when you call him. Go and find him. Take his collar in your hand. Lead him to the scene of his crime. Go into your act. SHAME ON YOU. DID YOU DO THAT? NO NO NO. BAD DOG. Bang your bare hand on the floor near his *crime.* Making a fuss beats beating your dog. It also gets the point across. The point is: If you use the outdoors, I'll be happy and praise you; if you use the indoors, I'll be angry and correct you.

Now, the hard part. After your display of displeasure, *you must walk the dog.* Human logic says, "What for? He just did what he had to do and he won't do it again. Besides, it's snowing." Dog logic says, "Hey, could you show me just one more time where you want me to do this." So, out with you both.

End to a Myth

Most books tell you that if you don't catch your dog in the act, you cannot correct him. With housebreaking, as well as a few other problems, this is untrue. Many dogs will only break the rules when you are not watching. Happily, they *can* be corrected because they leave evidence. When you remind a dog of his misdeed by showing him a wet spot or a messy blob on the rug, he'll recognize his own scent. He'll know the mess is his and not yours. Hence, if you march him over to it, show it to him (no noses rubbed in it—that's just sadistic) and make an angry display, he will get the message. Waiting for him to err in front of your watchful eyes can be unproductive and tedious, so do punish every housebreaking crime, even if no witnesses can be found.

Paper Training

All logic tells you not to paper-train your dog, yet sometimes there is simply no choice. He's little and hasn't had his shots. He cannot go out where other dogs go until he is inoculated. You are away too long at work and no one can get him out for a lunchtime walk. Then you must paper train.

Paper training, an accepted and classic method of housebreaking dogs, teaches the dog, on some subliminal level (the hard-to-get-to kind) that it's okay, if the circumstances are right, to eliminate indoors. This is my main objection to this method—and it isn't nit-picking. My second objection, which isn't chicken feed either, is that your dog will carry over the idea of wetting down paper long after the newspapers have been picked up from the kitchen floor. Drop a check when your dog is trying to catch your eye with that all-important message (You know the message: Help!), and you'll have to explain a wet or worse check to your local bank executive. So now you know why I think paper training should be avoided—if possible.

If not, line a whole small area, like a bathroom or a sectioned-off part of your kitchen, with several layers of newspaper. When doggy goes on the paper—and what on earth choice does he have when you think about it—praise him. Even praise him after the fact, when you get home from work. After a few days, begin to pick up the paper, starting at some obscure corner, a little at a time, making the papered area smaller. Furthermore, when you clean up, clean thoroughly. Put down fresh paper, several layers of it. Then take one wet sheet from the last round and place it on top of the clean papers in the corner where you want the paper bathroom to end up. This is the message: HERE! Each time you clean up, until your dog is aiming on target on about two sheets of the *Times*, five or seven sheets thick, leave a little message on the clean papers and work the papered area smaller in the direction you'd like it to go.

Now, when your little mess maker misses, you can correct him the way you would have if you were crate training—not by hitting, but by fussing somewhat and placing him, with praise, on the paper where he is supposed to go.

If you use this method and your dog is going to grow into something larger than a lima bean, pick up the papers as soon as you can, clean the floor with tons of ammonia, confine your dog in another room altogether and get him going outside on a tight walking schedule. If not, you'll be sorry. Don't forget you heard it here.

Sometimes, paper training creates an awful problem. The young puppy, never having eliminated outside, doesn't know that that's desirable or even permissible. He defies all records for holding, keeps his legs crossed, grits his teeth and after a two-hour walk—to no avail—bursts into the house and rushes to where his papers used to be. Problem? Problem!

Now you must use the crate, or a box, and confine the dog every minute he is indoors, so that he has no choice but to let go and sit in it or go outside. In fact, do not walk him from the crate to the yard or street. Carry him. Do not give him a chance to do anything but exactly what you want him to do. This can be a tough few days. One dear, confused Sheltie I worked with went for thirty-six hours before she anxiously let go outside to much praise. Incredibly, she did the same thing once again before getting the message. Understand that your dog is not acting out of spite or stupidity but is trying to please you and is very confused. At this point, firmness and guts are all that will get you both through.

Some people take soiled paper out and put it on the ground, anchored by rocks so that it won't blow away. They pray that the dog will get the message and that the neighbors will not see them. This sometimes works, but not always. Tight confinement and getting "flown" outside, all on a schedule, does work. It has to work within a couple of days. So, if you are stuck with this awful problem, do what you must to solve it and try not to have a nervous breakdown.

Litter-Box Training

If your dog is, in fact, going to remain the size of a lima bean or smaller, you may never want to walk it—or you may want to walk it once a day for exercise and fun, but not for purposes of elimination. In that case, many owners stick with paper training forever. A neater alternative is to use a litter box with kitty litter or newspaper in it. The box can be left someplace where the dog has access to it at all times and where you can easily keep it clean.

Training can be accomplished by a variety of routes. You can confine the dog in a small area containing his bed and the litter box. If he's only half as smart as you think he is, he should sleep in the bed and eliminate in the box. Correct him if he doesn't. Gradually make the area larger until he can negotiate over to his box when he needs it from anywhere in the house.

Alternately, you can keep the box out of the way, on the terrace or in the utility room, and take the dog to it, even on leash, following the walking schedule presented earlier. Praise him when he uses it and correct him if he uses your rug instead. The box should be kept clean or your dog won't want to put his tiny toes in it, but you *can* use a wet starter paper, as in paper training, to get the message through.

Port and Pen—the Protection Bonus

If you own your own home, dog walking can be solved in another interesting way. You can install an outdoor pen for the dog to use and have a dog port installed in the wall going from the house directly into the pen. Now, when you are gone all day, your dog can go out and relieve himself without waiting. Furthermore, if it rains or snows or is even too terribly hot, he won't be stuck outside in the pen, but can come in and get warm or dry or cool, as the case may be. There's an additional benefit from this setup. Although it's costly at first to buy the fencing and the port, your dog will not only be free to come and go when he needs to, but he will be able to protect your home, both inside and out. If you leave him in a pen, he is useless as a watchdog. If you keep him indoors for long hours, he'll be in physical discomfort. This convenient setup relieves you of keeping a tight or impossible schedule and allows the dog to function properly as a guardian of your home. While you surely should be able to sleep late or to have drinks after work without worrying about your dog's next walk, he should get out at least once a day for exercise and to keep him socialized.

Will a clever thief, spotting the port, enter the pen and then enter your home? If your dog is large enough to warrant a port big enough for a thief to crawl through, it would be a foolish thief indeed to try. Wouldn't you worry intensely about what you'd bump into on the other side of the port? Even the sight of the pen will alert potential thieves that there is a dog on the premises. Most would rather work elsewhere.

Dog Ports: Getting Your Dog Through

Occasionally, installing a dog port to solve problems creates a small, temporary problem of its own—getting your dog to use it. The solution is easy. If your port has a swinging door, affix it so that it stays open and your dog can see out to the deck, pen, patio, run or terrace. If your port is made of plastic triangles, do not install them into the frame for the first few days. Encourage your dog to go through the open port by clapping for him, calling him, praising him and offering food treats. You can have a member of the family or a friend on the other side of the port and take turns calling him back and forth, praising him each time. Leave the port open for a few days and close it gradually once he is easily going in and out. The door can be slowly lowered, affixing it at each new level for a day or two. If you have triangles, put one in at a time. Work with your dog at each step to keep his confidence up and make it fun to go through the port. Finally, with the opening closed, call him through with enthusiasm and reward him with a nice treat. Duck à l'orange is fine as long as the bones have been removed.

The Chronic Leg-Lifter

Here, for the first time, is a true problem dog—a pain in the neck, a scoundrel, a hardened criminal—the unhousebroken adult dog. He may be the dog you gave up trying to housebreak. He may be a five- or six- or seven-year-old who's been urinating on your furniture all these years. If you've told yourself stories (he'll outgrow it; he's dumb; he's spiteful), now is the time to stop.

Animals use their feces and urine as part of the way they communicate. If the dog you love is marking all over your house, there is a message in his madness. He is, first of all, claiming your territory as his own. He is, second of all, asserting himself over you as top dog. As if that weren't enough, he's urinating and defecating on you, too —via your possessions. Now that you understand the not-so-delicate truth, we can join forces and correct the chronic marker or the unhousebroken female who claims squatter's rights on your wall to wall.

Treat this problem as if it were an initial housebreaking problem with a puppy. *You must buy a crate.* At this point, nothing else will work. Confine your dog to the crate most of the time, as per the initial puppy schedule, unless he never has an accident—or an "on purpose," to be accurate—when you are home. If that is the case, confine him only and always when you are out. Since this is a chronic or long-term problem, there should be no rush to give your dog run of the house again. Initially, he was rewarded with freedom he did not deserve. Now he must lose that freedom entirely until he gives up this nasty habit. It will take time.

Most older dogs, after an initial fuss (one or two sessions of barking that may keep you awake for one or two nights), will accept the confinement of the crate. If your dog keeps making noise and your landlord threatens to evict you, consult The Noisy Dog (Chapter 8), and teach him to be quiet. Do not use his whining as an excuse to give up on his housebreaking. Think about where that might lead.

With a chronic leg-hiker, a crate and a tough attitude are both essential. You must stick to your guns, no matter what. If you start to let the dog roam about again before he is retrained, he will continue to soil your house. By using the crate and a schedule, you will prevent him from marking anything indoors unless you are watching. If he should err in front of your hawklike eyes, you will swoop down on him, shake him back and forth by his collar (his front paws move from side to side and his rear paws remain on the floor), make a huge display of anger, bang on the floor, SHAME SHAME him until he's blue in the face and walk him. Then, you'll come home with him and "find" the accident *again* and you will correct him all over again. After that, confine him in his crate until the next walk, giving him an icy shoulder to boot. Once this has been accomplished, clean the spot thoroughly. Leaving it for the next time or even for ten extra minutes past your second use of it delivers the opposite message from what you mean to send.

Either crate your dog and walk him on a schedule or, if you are sure he never marks when you are home, keep him in whatever room you are in—just to let him know Big Brother *is* watching him—and crate him when you leave, even for one minute. If all goes well for weeks and weeks, your house will begin to smell like *boeuf bourguignon* again instead of pee soup and you may begin to let the little brat have some freedom, a couple of minutes at a time. Do not rush him back to having the run of the house or he will immediately slide back to his old ways. Always check on him by checking his old favorite spots or walking barefooted on the rug. At any slip, even the tiniest—remember, he's a dog and he'll want to test—he loses *all* his freedom again for at least two weeks.

Expecting to go back and forth on this will keep you in a better frame of mind. It is also a good idea to run a fan at night when the dog is fussing in his crate. It will help block out the noise. I never promised you this would be easy—but I did promise you a rose garden, and your house will never come up smelling like roses if your dog reinforces his supremacy by urinating indoors—even if it's only on occasion. A housebroken dog would die before wetting indoors. In fact, when ill, dogs will slink and grovel in humiliation at having let go inside even though they physically could not help themselves.

Curing the chronic leg-lifter can take months and months. So what. During this time, your house is recuperating and he is forced to behave like a gentleman. With some willpower and patience on your part, he will eventually keep your territory clean and regain his run of the house. Remember, it was partly someone's poor communication with him previously that brought this problem about in the first place. Perhaps laziness added to the problem, so commit yourself now to going the whole hog or don't even begin. If you give up in the middle and let your smart little dog know he won a difficult battle, life will be far worse and he won't be long on the scene. Don't think for a minute that every movement, each dip and innuendo in your dominance dance, isn't clear to him. It is, it is. If you give up after starting, he'll know and take even more advantage of you as time goes by.

Submissive Urination

This is a clear-cut situation that you will have little trouble with once you understand it. The reasoning behind it gets into a rather sophisticated area of dog knowledge, so if you've goofed here, you're in good company. Luckily, it is a mistake that is easy to rectify.

If, when you come home from work, your dog runs to greet you at the door, tail wagging, ears down or back, hind leg tentatively lifting, observe. He may urinate, just a little, right where he is standing. He may roll over, instead, and urinate while exposing his belly to you. This is not technically an unhousebroken dog. Such behavior is a submissive display and urinating, in this case, is part of the language of submission—a white flag, so to speak. You should no more punish your dog than you would shoot a surrendering soldier.

Actually, your dog is just overreacting a little. Just coming to you, panting, wagging his tail and wiggling would be all the greeting you'd want. Your dog, however, feels the need to reassure you that you are top dog. The dog may be young, or a mild type, or you may be very assertive, large, gruff, powerful, masterful in your stance. Simply reassure the dog by talking gently and petting him. While you're at it, bend down to him, making your posture less aggressive. The sooner you do this upon greeting your dog, the faster you'll reassure him and the sooner he'll stop reassuring *you* by urinating. Don't make any kind of big deal about the few drops of urine. (Of course, do clean it up.) Just greet your dog quietly and pet him gently. Don't make a loud fuss or start roughhousing. In a sense, you're trying to make less of a big deal about your homecoming so that the dog can be more casual. But don't worry that he will become blasé about this all-important event. Even when he stops acting overly submissive and urinating, he'll still see you as top dog.

Housebreaking Accidents Due to Illness

Only a monster would correct a sick dog who just happened to ruin a new Flokati rug, right? Wrong.

If you allow your dog to begin a List of Reasons, you'll be in big trouble. If you allow Reason One, Illness, and Reason Two, Bad Weather, can you begin to imagine what he'll come up with? Whatever route he takes to get there, Reason Eight is bound to be: I felt like it. Accordingly, do correct your sick dog, but as mildly as possible. All you want to do is let him know that he's not supposed to evacuate body wastes indoors. Gently take him to the spot and tell him SHAME. You do not have to shake him or go on and on, but you do have to walk him. Since you now know he's sick, please walk him more often until the problem is cleared up—and watch more carefully for those messages: Help, Help, Help.

Scooping: Everything the Law Allows, and Then Some

If you and I and the guy down the block were good little dog owners last year and the year before, legislatures wouldn't be going crazy now writing laws about dog waste and designing those unattractive summonses. The best way to prevent a Scoop Law in your neighborhood, if it's not there already, is to pretend it is. When one really gives it some thought, it's clear that there is no other course of behavior for a responsible human than to clean up after one's dog. If you are not ingenious enough to find a creative and workable method of your own, and I can't believe that's true, just hang around my block any evening and watch how the dog owners in New York City have adapted and invented. Obeying the law is one step. Preventing additional legislation is the next. In crowded cities all over the United States, there are groups of people thinking of new ways to eliminate dog wastes. Many of them think that the best way to accomplish this is to eliminate the privilege of owning a dog in the city. Other groups suggest limiting the size of dog you may keep or the number you may own legally. If you and I want the freedom to determine for ourselves the number and size of dogs we may keep, it's best to be not just legal, but exemplary. How you choose to do that—to upgrade the negative image of dogs and their owners —is really up to you. For all the pleasure our dogs give us, it's really worth a try. If we don't, who will?

4

Larceny—Petty and Grand

Why do you rob banks?
Because that's where the money is.

—Willy Sutton

If you drop a piece of chicken onto the kitchen floor and before you can say "Butterfingers!" your dog ingests it, that is not stealing.

If, while you're getting dressed to go to work, your dog sneaks into your room, where he normally is not allowed, grabs a piece of underwear and takes off to play catch-me-if-you-can behind the dining room table, that is stealing.

A little Fox Terrier I knew was fascinated by the sound paper cups made coming out of the dispenser. No sooner did her owners leave for work than she would leap an astonishing height and, one at a time, with the patience, but not the behavior, of a saint, pull out each and every cup and drop it to the floor. She didn't chew them. As far as anyone could tell, she didn't even play with them. Occasionally, she'd let passion rule and, even when someone was home, out of sight and out of mind in another room, the familiar pop pop pop of the paper cups leaving the dispenser would be heard. Stealing? Stealing.

Shauna, after a brief career as a couch eater, didn't touch anything of value in the house, which was a great relief to her owners, but for ages and ages she'd pirate paper from the wastebaskets and tear it up. Many unspayed females steal paper and shred it. Some steal and shred only right before coming into heat. Others will occasionally tear up a section of the newspaper when they are neither coming into heat nor expecting puppies, just to keep in practice. Stealing? I think not. This behavior seems to be part of the nesting instinct.

Many dogs steal hats or gloves from little kids they love. Sometimes they do this to begin a game, sometimes to have a little amulet with the wonderful odor of a loved one permeating it, sometimes to get a little attention. Lots of dogs steal clothing from the bedroom floor or the laundry basket and play chase or just parade around. Some destroy their prize. Some just try to keep it as long as they can. And what dog, tall enough to reach table or counter, grew up without stealing a steak, a chicken, a bread—whatever's there—when your back is turned. Stealing? You bet.

Does the canine thief steal, or do anything else for that matter, out of spite? Most owners think dogs do behave spitefully. Most people who work with animals or study their behavior think they don't. *Your* answer to this question is important because it will color the way you handle your misbehaving dog.

While appearances seem to stack up in favor of spite as a motive, the facts go against it. Dogs are usually very direct in their behavior. A dog who wants to be petted will come up to you and put his head in your lap or under your hand; a dog who wants to play will bring his ball. Your dog may watch your steak like an owl watches a mouse—and when you crawl into bed and he wants to join you, doesn't he let you know how he feels?

Spite is an indirect form of anger. Unlike a bite or a fight, which would expel anger, spite doesn't satisfy. It is almost self-perpetuating. Unfortunately for us, it is very much the way humans learn to behave. Prevented from expressing anger in many situations, we try to satisfy ourselves with gossip, wisecracks and spite. We redirect, we become indirect when we cannot be simple and straightforward, like our dogs. But the modus operandi of the dog is easy, direct and clear.

What appears to be spiteful behavior—stealing when he knows he shouldn't, urinating on the bed, tearing up the furniture when left alone—is often motivated by anxiety. You cannot tell your dog when you'll be back—or even *that* you'll be back. He cannot read the clock and figure out when his next meal is coming. Every minute, to a dog, is forever. Often, he doesn't know where he's going or when he's coming home or how long you'll be gone. It's no wonder he's subject to anxiety.

A dog's anxiety can be relieved by contact, by petting and cuddling, and by discipline, by a return to a clear pecking order and sensible pack regulations. It is, then, sometimes his need for reassurance that causes him to misbehave. It's his clumsy way of saying, "You person, me dog. Right?" If contact and discipline can *allay* anxiety, is it fair to assume that their absence can *cause* it? I think so.

Let's return to the dog who steals underwear. You are getting ready to leave for work. After all, you've got to earn a living. To your dog, who knows nothing of bills and mortgages, this means another slapdash walk around the block (he may even hold out on you to hang onto you a little longer), a breakfast with hardly so much as a how-do-you-do and another boring day at home all alone.

He's not aware of your needs, your problems. All he knows is that you're doing those dozen things you do before leaving the house and that he better do something fast to draw attention to himself before it's too late. Attention. That's the key.

A lot of stealing is done to get attention and to gain time. I'm not saying he's right. I'm not saying you have the time to give him. I'm not even saying you have to make the time. Not yet, anyway. All I'm saying is that his need for contact, for a challenge, for fun and games, for attention, is a much more plausible reason for his behavior than spite. And if you understand it *this* way instead of *that* way, you'll feel a lot more moved to work on the *cause* as well as the symptoms than you would if spite were his burning motive. After all, how sympathetic can you feel toward someone who is spiting you.

Spite is nasty business, but most dogs are not nasty creatures. Those few that are will have a lot worse things going for them than stealing socks and panties. Those culprits we'll get to later. For now, there's no harm done if we make the assumption that your dog is a sweetheart with a problem you now understand and so can begin to correct.

Object-Stealing for Attention

Most often, when your dog runs off with an object not his, it's something special. It may be your child's favorite teddy, in which case it is imbued with your child's wonderful (to your dog, that is) smells. Your dog may be trying to steal the special attention your child is getting or the special attention the teddy is getting, or he may just want this wonderful object for his own. He, too, likes to have something delicious and sweet to cuddle and call his own. Many dogs, just like little kids, will fall asleep with a favored toy under head or paw. Of course, your child won't appreciate any of Fido's reasons. It's *his* teddy, and that's that. So you must find a way to keep Fido away from teddy.

Your dog may have an aversion to teddy bears. He might prefer dirty socks and underwear. That's his business. It becomes yours when he hits and runs for attention, when he steals to entice you into a game of tag. Even the negative attention his panty raid might call down upon him may still be worth it. It's not the object that's important here (each dog to his own taste), but the larceny must be stopped.

There is no one best or perfect way to stop stealing. As with many other problems, it's all right to begin with one correction and experiment until you find the one that works best—that is, the one your dog dislikes enough so that he amends his behavior to avoid it. As with all dog training, always *use the softest correction that works.* There's no need to beat a dog when a simple NO, NO would do the trick. Start slowly.

First, prepare to replace what your dog steals with something it's all right for him to have. Whenever possible, it's preferable to make a correction complete and have it end on a positive note. For example: "No, you can't chew my slipper, but—good news—here's a piece of rawhide you can chew." That's the Serendipitous Method. Your satisfied dog will find it much easier to be obedient. This does not mean that a chunk of food should replace stolen objects. You'd then be *rewarding* the act of stealing, rather than replacing the stolen object with an acceptable one. Food, a classic animal reward tool, doesn't last. So, instantly, your dog, clever little character, will be out stealing again—now for the double reward: the fun and thrill of larceny plus the food treat it brings.

There are many creative ways to stop dogs from swiping things. You can set up some temptation rather than waiting for him to steal when you are most busy and harried. Drop a nice sock on the floor, the very one you jogged eight miles in. Now let's work with strings attached. Attach one to the sock—or one to your dog. Either way, you're in control. If the string is on the sock, tell him NO, OUT as he grabs it and begins his fifty-yard dash. Now either walk down the string to the dog or just give a yank as you repeat OUT. This depends largely on how tightly he clamps his jaws on his treasure. If need be, follow down the string, hand over hand, then clasp his jaw over the top, saying OUT. If he won't open his mouth, apply a little pressure, pressing his cheeks onto his teeth. His mouth will open. Remove your smelly, now wet sock, *praise your dog*, give him one of his toys and praise him again.

Although it may seem peculiar, a dog should be praised for any behavior you want him to repeat, even if, this time, you forced him to do it entirely against his will. Thus, when you force his jaws open, you praise him just as if he gave up his prize all on his own. Then, one day, he will. Also, he's smart, but not *that* smart, so when you praise him for something he's just done, he feels mighty pleased. He likes the feeling. It's as if he thinks, "I'm good? I'm good! I did something marvelous. I'm terrific." You can bamboozle a dog in a very nice way by praising him enthusiastically for doing something *you made him do* and thus you can make him *think* he did it all by himself and is deserving of all that praise. After all, it *is* logical. If he didn't deserve it, why would you deliver it?

After a few of these sessions, you may be able to get away with a strong NO, OUT just as he's about to take off. If not, tie a string or cord to his collar and set up an opportunity for him to steal. Now you can call him to come when he's taking off with his prize. He won't? That's why there's a string. Pull the string. Result? One dog, one sock. Remove the sock. Praise the dog. Give the dog a toy of his own.

After a few of these sessions, don't call the dog to come. When he steals the sock, hold the string and go to your dog. Take his collar in your hand and shake him back and forth so that his front end moves from side to side and his rear end remains in contact with the ground. As you shake him back and forth, three or four times, tell him NO, NO, NO. Command OUT in a firm, annoyed, businesslike voice and remove the sock. Give him his toy and praise him, but do not be overly friendly. It's time to get serious about all this stealing. After all, a sock is just a sock, but we might be dealing with a teddy bear. Teddy bears are serious.

While you are shaking up your dog's routine and trying to teach him a new, more acceptable one, let's think again about his behavior as a bid for attention. Your kids are leaving for school, you are leaving for work. Or it's bedtime and you are giving all your attention to your children. Who has the time and energy to deal with a demanding dog? You do—or you wouldn't have gotten this far. If your dog is obedience-trained, this is the time to capitalize on that previous work. Use an obedience command to give your dog the feeling he's being useful, terrific and smart. Thus, he'll be working, using his brain, getting praised and getting the attention he was after in the first place. You don't have the time to take him out and heel him for half an hour? Then, after his normal walk, heel him for five minutes, just to warm him up. Bring him inside and, while you go about your business, put your dog on a DOWN, STAY. As you move from room to room, release him, praise him and move him with you. It won't take more than a few seconds of your time, far less than chasing him with your attaché case dangling from his mouth and all your papers flying. If he's on a ten-minute DOWN, you are free for ten minutes, and he is working for ten minutes—and happy to do so.

There are many other ways to give your dog a little more attention without quitting your job or putting your children up for adoption. Have the kids play with the dog. Have the kids groom and brush the dog. You or they can brush him while you watch television. If your dog is an energetic little roughneck, toss a ball for him while you are doing something else—or nothing else. If you get him to bring it back as part of the game, you can do it while lounging in a Morris chair—or a tub full of bubbles.

One bitch I trained loved to carry around socks and undies. One day, watching her, I got a brainstorm. Her owner was in the middle of collecting dirty clothes for the wash. Lulu had grabbed a sock and, tail wagging, was parading around with it. I called her to come. I told her OUT. The sock dropped onto the laundry pile. Then I pointed to one of the kid's rooms and told her GO FIND ANOTHER ONE. By the time we were through, Lulu had carted in all the laundry from all the bedrooms and dropped each piece onto the pile in the bathroom. She was delighted. While it would have taken less effort for her owner to pick up all the dirty clothes herself, this was much more fun and it let Lulu feel productive and happy.

You can get this kind of double mileage out of your time by observing what your dog likes to do naturally. Then name it and use it. Many dogs are absolute nuts for both carrying things and finding things. If your dog is stealing, he already likes carrying things around in his mouth, so it would make a lot of sense, while correcting this as a bad habit, to reroute this desire into a trick or game. While discouraging him from carrying around your clothes or your children's toys, you can work with him and encourage him to carry around a ball or small purse, an eyeglass case or key ring. Then, if so moved, you can start referring to the object by name and sending him to find it when you're busy and he's not.

Now, when you are getting ready for work, send your dog on a scavenger hunt. The time it takes you will be minimal, yet it may take your dog all of breakfast time to find his key ring. He'll not feel neglected and left out. He'll not feel so deserted when you leave. He'll be brighter and more fun because you turned a bad habit into a useful skill. *That* is the definition of the Serendipitous Method of training dogs.

Stealing Garbage

People are often surprised at my method for stopping a dog from stealing garbage. I explain that there are two ways. The dog, having a far better sense of smell than we do, will be tempted by all those yummy, rotting things in the garbage. It really is difficult for him to resist chicken bones and pungent cheese, roast beef fat and bacon drippings. Most dogs eventually give in to temptation. You can beat your dog every time he does it—and hope he gets the point and stops before the chicken bones kill him—or you can put the garbage away, in a can with a lid or stashed under the sink. I like the second method.

Of course, when I am cooking and need a garbage bag out for convenience, I take the opportunity to correct my dog with a simple, firm NO if he sniffs near the garbage or peeks into the bag. In time, this soft correction is usually enough to work while you are home or around. However, for safety, simplicity and even neatness, I do keep the kitchen garbage can under the sink, behind closed doors. Prevention is excellent dog training. It is also very *easy* dog training and I am as lazy as the next person.

Stealing Food

Stealing food can be considered a major crime, especially when added to the crime of the price we have to pay for it lately. With the cost of living rapidly rising, disappearing steaks and chops can no longer be considered cute. While it is normal for a dog to try, food stealing can be stopped.

When six hungry guests are drinking and starving in your living room and you are putting the final touches to your chilled apricot soup and duck in red wine sauce, it's a poor time to have to correct a pilfering dog. If your formal dinner party is tonight, stop reading, confine light-fingered Louie in the bedroom with a supply of rawhide and a farewell pat on the head and get thee to the kitchen. You may be using instant wild rice, but there is no instant dog training.

This aspect of your dog's training should take place, as much as possible, when you have the time and the energy. Of course, while he's still an uneducated clod, your dog will go after your chicken Kiev or your chicken à la Colonel whenever you turn your back, so you will have to be careful along the way and keep an eagle eye on old Louie. Then, we will set up temptations, follow through and hope for the best. I prefer using salami as bait rather than filet mignon. Your choice will depend on the size of *your* royalty checks.

Before beginning, we must give some thought to the matter of communication. Sure, if you pull your dog off the counter where the lamb chops are defrosting, saying NO, NO, NO, he'll know something's up. But there is an easy, practical step that should come first. Your dog should learn not to take *any* food, even the stuff in his own dish, without permission. This will not only speed up your communication in teaching him not to steal food, but it is great for stopping him from ingesting Good Humor wrappers in the street and old bubble gum off the elevator floor. It will help you have control over what goes into your dog, including at dinner parties, in the park and back in the kitchen. It may, for a small amount of effort, not only hasten the end of a stealing problem but, better still, prevent a case of poisoning and lots of bellyaches.

Begin by saying OK whenever you give your dog anything to eat. Put down his food bowl or hand him a biscuit, say OK in a bright voice and praise him when he eats. He won't know what's going on yet—but he's beginning to get the message subliminally. That's exactly what we want. Do this for a week, making sure that everyone who has anything to do with the dog tells him OK when he gets something to eat.

Week Two is here. Hold out a biscuit, saying nothing. When he opens his mouth, tell him NO. He will look puzzled. However, if he hesitates, even a second, tell him OK, give him the biscuit and praise him. Of course, he is getting a double reward for waiting—food and praise. That is fine in this case. We are teaching him not to take food until he gets the release word OK. By now, all those OK's you gave him last week are creeping slowly toward the surface of his consciousness. Again, offer a biscuit (no speeches—just hold it out). If he hesitates at all, tell him OK and let him take it. If he's very sensitive, you might have to tell him OK, GOOD BOY. Then he'll know it's *really* OK. If he grabs, don't let him have it. Wait for him to wait—but don't push. This is not an exercise in macho. Two seconds are preferable to two minutes right now. After all, anyone can bully a dog into not taking a cookie. That is not the point.

Try this a few more times, occasionally offering the biscuit and saying OK so that it doesn't just become a routine or a trick. That will make him listen and think. If he's rather soft and quick to learn, place the last biscuit on the floor. If he waits and maybe drools a little, give him an enthusiastic OK, praise him and end the session.

Continue to use the OK for all food but practice the NO only two to three times a week. In this case, more is not better than less. If you work very hard at this, your dog may get very neurotic, never knowing when he can just relax and eat and when he can't. After a while, your patience will be rewarded and he will begin to understand that he is not to consider food unless he hears his OK. Teaching NO and OK for food will help a lot in breaking him from stealing, but it will not do the job by itself. It is, however, so easy and so useful that it is worth teaching even to dogs who do not steal. One caution should be mentioned. If your dog is not a puppy and is very aggressive or has already bitten, it would be wiser to eliminate this training, at least until the more serious problems are under control.

Now that your dog has the right idea about which delicious goodies he has rights to and which ones you have all dibs on, you can begin to tempt him into stealing when you don't have dinner guests waiting in the living room. As with NO and OK for food, do not practice this more than two or three times a week on purpose, but do correct your dog for infringing on your food when he does it on his own.

Take a piece of salami (it has an odor he can't miss) and put it on a little dish on the counter or on your kitchen table. Now putter about, pretending to be preoccupied—but keep an eye on your dog. His mouth is fast, as well you know, but your hand has to be faster. If you set up the salami and he keeps getting it, you will be making him much worse instead of putting an end to his bad habit.

Try the following corrections when he tries for the salami. Try a loud NO. If he backs away, empty-mouthed, praise him. Leave the salami for one or two more forays. If the phone rings, put the salami in the fridge or eat it. Your attention won't be on Louie and he'll be the first to know it. Once you are off the phone, put another piece of salami on the counter. Now Louie makes his move. This time, grab his collar and pull him back off the counter, not too gently. Tell him NO, BAD LOUIE. Now, fill your plant mister or, if you prefer, your kid's water gun. To begin, use plain water. When Louie's paws surround the salami, shoot him in the nose. If water doesn't shock him, surprise him, discourage him one drop, lace the water with white vinegar, one tablespoon per gun load, or two or three in the plant mister if it is large. Now shoot for the nose-mouth area, avoiding the dog's eyes.* This correction will work on many dogs and has the added advantage of working from a distance. The dog may not be sure where the annoying surprise came from, nor if it would come with you out of the room.

In all this work, you must be prepared, if your dog's mouth should prove quicker than your hand, to pounce upon the dog, pry open his jaws and retrieve the salami. While it is not entirely necessary to commit suicide if you lose a piece or two along the way, allowing Louie to eat the salami does do great harm to the training. Each piece of food he steals and ingests reinforces the activity you are working to stop. Unless your dog is very growly and protective over his food, you should be pretty safe opening his mouth and digging out his loot. You will, after all, have the element of surprise on your side. Besides, having paid for all the food he stole already, you should have enough adrenalin on your side to pull it off even if your pet is considerably larger than a breadbox.

One additional caution: Many frustrated owners, once the dog has dragged the five-pound sirloin to the kitchen floor, punish him wildly and then let him have the steak back, figuring that no one

---

* Consultation with a veterinary opthalmologist, confirmed that use of diluted vinegar is deemed safe for most dogs. In cases of individual susceptibility, discontinue the use of diluted vinegar if eyes seem irritated. Rinse eyes with plain water and consult your veterinarian. This irritation will be of short duration and will not cause permanent damage.

else would eat it now anyway. While the premise is true enough, Louie has gotten a mammoth reward for his light-fingered larceny. Please do not reward your dog for stealing by letting him enjoy the fruits of his labors. If you hate wasting food, give the steak to the nice dog next door who doesn't steal.

Object-Stealing and -Guarding

There are some dogs who steal odd things of seemingly no value at all and guard their treasures with their lives. One lady Malamute I knew would steal rags or dish towels, hover over her prize as if it were a newborn pup and growl if anyone approached her. If she wasn't guarding, she was a pretty nice dog, but you'd never know when that crazy notion would get into her head.

Object-guarding often borders on the neurotic. Sometimes it does more than border—it drowns in it. If your dog goes ape over rags or bones or a particular toy, first get rid of the thing that triggers the action and see what happens next. Often a dog that displays this sort of scary, erratic behavior is really a problem dog, a dog who does not understand what he may truly keep, and when, a dog whose protective instincts are hair-trigger and inappropriate, an insecure and fearful dog who may bite at any time.

Often, a dog who displays erratic behavior—you know, the Jekyll and Hyde of the canine world—is a dog for whom no clear limits have been set. Sometimes it means that the owner has been arbitrary and inconsistent, correcting much too harshly for an offense one day and letting the same thing go unnoticed the next. Thus, erratic upbringing has produced erratic behavior in the dog. He, too, is overreacting one day and being passive the next. The trouble with that is that *you* never know what will set him off—just as he never knew what would set *you* off.

When a dog makes a life-or-death stand over a rag or a half-chewed toy in the bosom of the family that loves him, no matter what the cause, that is crazy behavior. The dog may be very neurotic because of bad breeding, or he may be expressing his fear and nervousness caused by any number of things that could have happened before you two met. Your actions could have made the situation worse or better or had little effect on it. At any rate, even if you precipitated this behavior, you probably did it in all innocence and with the best intentions in the world. Blaming yourself now will not do much to help the dog.

If your dog is already obedience-trained, carefully examine your attitudes and level of consistency when dealing with the dog and giving commands. Training should be tightened, firmly and gradually. The dog must obey a command each time it is issued and should be praised each time he obeys. Opportunity for stealing should be pared down to a minimum. Get rid of all objects to which the dog has formed these crazy attachments. They can only bring trouble. Try, at least until new habits are formed, to think about what you do concerning the dog. Consistency is the key word. Be doubly sure the dog is exercised as much as possible, and then some. Swimming is one of the best ways to rid a dog of ants in the pants. A well-exercised dog is less likely to walk around looking for trouble.

Consistency and tighter training will give the dog the limits and rules he needs, but he must also be clear about *his* rights. This lack of clarity may also be reflected in object-guarding. The kids should not fuss with this dog's food or toys and he should have a routine that is fairly rigid and totally predictable. He also needs a place of his own where he can sleep or chew a bone undisturbed.

Like the bully we all grew up fearing, your dog may be covering cowardice with aggression. However, in dealing with a dog, don't count on the fact that the layer of aggression is a thin one and that the dog will readily back down. That is probably not the case. You had a better chance, though you probably didn't know it then, of backing down your old block bully than your old growling dog.

If you are afraid of your dog (and you may have good reason to be), you may require the help of a professional dog trainer. In any case, the future looks grim in any situation where the owner is afraid and a dog is acting aggressive. It might be wise to set a reasonable time limit on trying to correct the problem, with the knowledge that, if it doesn't ameliorate during that time, it will be necessary to put the dog to sleep. Sadly, he cannot be offered as a pet to anyone else. Passing him around would only make matters worse and would jeopardize the safety of another family.

5

Begging, Tugging, Jumping, Sneaking Up on Furniture, Dogs in Bed

The best way to escape from a problem is to solve it.

—Brendan Francis

Begging and How To Resist It

You know the routine—and it's a knockout! Innocent eyes, brows turned upward, mouth in a pout. Suddenly, drool. The sympathy it provokes! The rewards it brings!

For many dogs, begging is a full-time job. They take their careers very seriously. What else do they have to do? Dogs being dogs, they'll persist forever if there's even a hint of reward. If your dog is begging for tidbits, chances are that someone feeds him at the table or that you give him table food at the end of the meal. Something is motivating all that hard work. Begging doesn't usually get very far if it is not rewarded.

Some find begging cute. Others find it irritating. If you fall into the second category, you'll find begging rather easy to stop. You can put your dog in another room when you dine. You can put your trained dog on a DOWN, STAY. Mealtime is a terrific time to practice obedience work and this is just the command that will do the trick. You cannot feed the dog from the table. If there are leftovers you want him to have, you can bag them, refrigerate them and add them to his morning chow. That will help stop begging and help prevent an obesity problem.

Suppose you *like* the begging routine. Think Serendipity. Teach the dog to beg properly, as a trick. It's classic. It's cute. Most dogs learn rapidly to sit up and beg for a tidbit of food. You can use a broken-up dog biscuit for the tidbits and entertain your kids and your company. All this, which will thrill your dog, will increase your rapport with him as well. Any education does that.

Suppose you're like me (I love to feed my dog at the table). When company comes, though, I tell my dog GO LIE DOWN. He then repairs to another area and reclines until the meal is over. Classy! Instructions for this handy command are in Chapter 10.

Begging is not a serious offense, though it may offend some seriously, but it can evoke some serious thinking about dogs and humans and the many ways in which they interact. Dogs, being dependent on us, become remarkably adept at manipulating us. If something fails, they drop it. If it works, they play it to the hilt. If you are a sucker for limpid eyes, your dog will know it and he'll use that knowledge to his distinct advantage. Can you blame him?

If you just can't say "No," you'll be feeding your obese dog all kinds of junk food, you'll never leave the house without him, you'll be sleeping on a tiny portion of your own bed and you'll only be able to stretch out on the couch if you get there first. Things can get out of hand.

If you've got the upper hand, if you're not stuck with a dog mooning at you whenever you eat, if your dog is a five-mile-a-day jogger, by all means feed him whenever you like. Let him bite your hamburger and chomp on your apple. But if his begging is only one of a whole set of problems, then it's time to look at the forest and forget about one tree. A perfectly nice dog who begs because he has been rewarded with food is one thing. A dog who begs because he's spoiled and won't listen to anyone and over whom you have little control is another. Treat the first, if you like, to a tidbit. The second one needs rules, more training and a firmer hand, not table food.

Tugging

Tugging is one of those odd activities your dog has a desire to do. If he tugs on your bathrobe, your children's clothing, the laundry you are carrying in the laundry basket, you will be unhappy. You can help him reroute this desire to pull things with his powerful jaws, in such a way that you have control and he is having fun without doing harm. Here is the perfect opportunity to use the Serendipitous Method of problem solving and satisfy the drive your dog is expressing while still getting rid of an annoying problem.

Your dog is a very oral character. While he may not take to cigarettes and chewing gum, he would happily spend a great deal of his awake time gnawing on a bone. He loves and needs to use his jaws in many ways, ways that were connected once, long ago, to the survival of his kind. Now, while these drives still exist, they may seem to you like just so many dinosaurs. Yet most dogs like using their mouths on more than food and bones. They like to tug and pull, and given no alternatives, may do so on your ticklish toes or your children's socks, caps and mittens. Many will grab hold of the leash and pull at it during a walk. This little habit is double-edged. Your trained dog knows the power of the leash, both the instrument and symbol of your control over him; he is not merely exercising his jaws in a harmless way. It may be his cute way of taking over command and control.

Of course, you do not want your dog controlling the leash. Nor do you want him tugging at your children and tearing their corduroys and ski jackets. If you have more than one dog, you'll probably find that they have reinvented the tug-of-war. If you're lucky, they'll do it with an old rope or a stick, but some dogs, in want of ropes and sticks, will settle for couch pillows, scarves, leather jackets, or any other item they can get their mouths on.

By all means, stop your dog from any offensive or destructive tugging. Grasp his collar and tell him NO, OUT. Repeat this correction each time he tries. If necessary, after two or three corrections, confine him for a while if he won't stop. Don't wait to work on the other side of this problem until he's all trained. While you are in the process of teaching him what *not* to pull, get him something he *can* tug and work on acceptable tugging. It won't confuse him. It will teach him more rapidly. It will satisfy his strong drive. It will make him more fun and more interesting for you to play with—all for the same small effort.

You can use a knotted rope or figure-eight dog toy. Entice your dog to tug, using the words TUG IT, TUG IT with enthusiasm.

Keep teaching the words and praising as you give your dog a run for his money. Then, after he's had a chance to tug really hard for a few minutes, freeze, tell him OUT and stop pulling against him. You have not only added an active, pleasant game to your dog's repertoire, but since he knows NO, you can now string together two of his vocabulary words when the situation warrants it. The result? NO TUG. Your control is improving daily and his brain is making astonishing connections.

Jumping Up

When dogs jump up on people, uninvited and unexpected, it usually causes more embarrassment to the owner than pain to the victim. However, when the dog's chosen object is a child, an elderly person, someone who is afraid of dogs or anyone caught totally by surprise, the results are worse than you getting a bit red in the face. Many dogs are powerful enough to knock someone down, to soil or tear clothes and to deliver a bad scare. Your dog, even if he's little, should not bounce off people when he feels exuberant and enthusiastic about saying hello. He can learn gentler ways to deliver a greeting.

Your dog will continue an act that gives *him* pleasure. If it doesn't please you, frankly, he couldn't care less. Being no dummy, he will discontinue an act that always brings him displeasure. When results are a mixed bag, he's apt to take his chances and hope for the best. When it comes to gambling, your dog is very willing to put his money on a long shot. So, to stop his jumping, consistency is the key.

If one out of ten of your friends is enchanted with the wild and crazy greeting your dog delivers ("Oh, look! He loves me"), they will project that to the dog. They don't even have to *pet* him. He'll feel their enthusiasm, pleasant surprise and gratitude. His jumping will have been reinforced positively. The winning card is still up your sleeve, though, not your dog's. When company comes, you'll know it. The bell will ring, the doorman will call up, the car will pull into your driveway, you'll hear a knock or, if worse comes to worst, your dog will bark. Simply keep a leash near the front door and snap it onto your dog's collar before you open the door. You can call through the door and briefly mumble something about training your dog if the procedure embarrasses you, but it shouldn't. It's what happens if you don't break this habit that is really embarrassing.

Now, dog on leash, brace yourself and open the door. As your dog begins his jump, jerk back on the leash, tossing him completely out of range and out of the way, saying NO JUMPING. Keep the leash loose enough so that he is free to make the mistake of trying to jump and tight enough so that when you pull him back he doesn't go flying. This is a *controlled toss*. You are not throwing the dog and allowing him to land where he may. He may possibly jump again, depending on his breed, age, sex and personality. If he does, you will correct him again. Tell him to sit and have your visitor, if willing, pet and greet the dog. Now twin messages are coming through. Your dog is learning that a paws-on greeting will be interrupted by an unpleasant correction and that a polite, sitting hello will be rewarded by kind words and petting.

The corrections for jumping are not difficult. However, they do require you to have the dog and the problem in mind. Each time you open your door to guests or family, your dog must be on leash so that you can use the opportunity for training him. When you forget and he can have the fun of a bounce-off-the-belly greeting, you go back three giant steps. Remember his penchant for long shots. While this training is easier to do than dipping your arm down his throat to retrieve the chicken he stole, it will take a long time. You are dependent upon callers to trigger his desire to jump and upon your making good use of these chances for reeducating your dog.

Now, what happens when he jumps on you? The leash correction is the most controlled, the most effective and the easiest to do. However, there are several others and you should use them all. They are not only practical when you are alone or cannot manage a leash correction for some other reason, but they are also valuable in that they add the elements of variety and surprise to your dog work. He will not be able to predict you, therefore he cannot learn to sidestep you. He will, of necessity, have to mend his ways.

When you come home and your dog begins to greet you, paws first, you have a few choices for correcting him. You can raise your knee so that as he raises his body, you bump him in the chest. As you do this, say NO JUMPING. Ask him to sit and praise him. Or you can, if you are fast, slip your hand into his collar as he jumps on you and jerk him off balance sideways. You may get hit with his paws in the process, but *c'est la vie*. Do not let go of the collar until you place your dog on the ground. Again, as you correct him, teach him the words NO JUMPING. They will begin to work on their own after a few weeks of physical corrections. They also add to your communication with your dog.

If your dog is too short for a knee in the chest and too short for you to slip your hand easily into his collar without much bending, simply slide your foot along the floor so that you unbalance him. Do not step on his feet, just slide gently into them and keep shoving so that he must put his front paws down to regain balance. Grab the collar and tell him SIT. Greet him calmly while he's sitting so that you reinforce the behavior you desire.

It is a good idea, though not entirely necessary, to enlist the help of friends in these corrections. At the very least, they should not greet the dog back nor pet him when he jumps up. They should not, nor should you, pat their own chests or legs and ask the dog to jump up. If your dog jumps on them and gets loved for it, he will continue trying to jump on everyone. If your friends are understanding and able, teach them one or two of the other corrections so that they can help you get the message through.

Even if you are a semi-recluse, you will have other blue chip opportunities to turn your bouncing dog into a good citizen. He may be one of those excitable, friendly types who tries to jump on everyone in the street. If so, you can use the leash correction and have each walk be a lesson as well. Just practice first and be sure you can pull him back before he plants his gigantic, muddy paws on some perfectly nice, well-dressed stranger.

While opportunities for correction abound, this bad habit is usually slow to retreat. If you understand that, it will be easier on you and your dog. It will require a commitment to be consistent and patient. Eventually, your dog will greet all comers with wagging tail, four on the floor and no surprises.

Sneaking Up on Furniture

Sneaking up on the furniture while you are away from home is not the worst thing a dog could do. Nor is it the best. Very often, the dog who reclines all day on the couch is not a problem dog. He is, instead, a very nice dog. This may be his only fault. Yet, if he is large and oily or even small and curly, he can bring a perfectly good couch to near ruin in no time. He may picnic up there, try to bury a bone or just give himself a bath and make your velvet couch stained and stiff.

If your dog goes up on the furniture while you are home, you can easily correct him. Tell him NO, OFF. Grasp his collar and fly him to the floor. He may feel he's in free flight, but, of course, he's not. You are not throwing him, just tossing him off with complete control, not releasing his collar until all four of his paws are safely on the floor. We never want to harm a dog in making a correction. Several unscheduled flights should do the job—when you are around. However, the dog may still prefer furniture to floor while you are out.

Now you have a decision to make—one that deals with training, pecking order, lifestyle and even compassion. You can give your dog his way, if that's what you really want. You can stop this habit if it displeases you. Your decision will depend on what your dog lies on, how much it cost, how old it is anyway, how old the dog is and how you like your home to look.

My client, Adele, has a Golden Retriever who very much liked to be on the couch. Even at-home corrections didn't discourage him. The brute, large indeed for a Golden, tipped the scales at ninety-two pounds. Adele, though not a cleaning nut, ran a tight ship. She did not want Raffles on the couch. She heard about the mousetrap method. Place mousetraps under newspaper. Dog puts paws up, mousetraps go off. Noise scares dog. *Voilà!* Since she didn't want the nice man in the hardware store to think she had mice or something like that, she had to be more inventive. She knew that when a dog goes up on furniture, it is after something warm and soft and maybe even with your nice odor on it, so she covered the seat of the couch with aluminum foil. It was cold, had no pleasant smells and wasn't comfortable at all. With no further work, Raffles, the world's stubbornest Golden, gave up after a week or two. Be inventive. That's good dog training.

My daughter's Shepherd mix, Bosco, never went up on the furniture until he was ten years old. By then, his thermostat was not functioning very well. When he felt cold, he'd cuddle on the couch. He knew it was an evil thing to do, yet comfort called. I knew he was up there because I found hair and saliva spots. The couch was still warm when I came home, to add insult to injury. The couch was getting ruined, but I don't have the heart to punish a dog that old, so, whenever I left the house, I tossed the floor pillows onto the couch. I didn't care if Bosco went up there on them. I saved the couch. I felt both satisfied and humane. Tougher-hearted trainers would have corrected the dog. I tend to get looser when dogs reach their golden years.

You can confine your dog in the kitchen, but this will only postpone the problem—it won't solve it. Two years later, he may still go on the furniture if you let him out when you aren't in. If it's okay with you to confine him when you aren't home, it's okay with me. This is merely a matter of lifestyle. We are not dealing with a major war crime, like biting, which must be stopped.

You can, as I did, cover the couch. It's annoying. Sometimes you forget. Sometimes the couch gets hairy. And, yes, it's not great dog training, but it's okay. I like to save my greatness for important things.

You can, when you come home to a hot seat on the couch, chair or bed, march your dog over to it, bang on the furniture (not on the dog) and chew him out. He knows he was up there. You've brought him back to the scene of his crime and he can smell his own scent. You can shove the pillow he was lying on in his face. You can tell him NOOOOO when he approaches the couch when you are home. Whatever you do, you must be consistent. He can't sit up there and watch TV with you and then be expected to stay on the floor the rest of the time.

When bad behavior is part of a syndrome or package that shows us, bit by bit, that the dog sees himself as top dog, we are dealing with something that is potentially dangerous and must be handled straight and square. When dealing with annoying habits that don't endanger your life or the dog's, you can have a softer attitude without harming anything except maybe your checkbook or your self-image of perfection. Since no one's perfect anyway, you can no more expect yourself to be than you can expect your dog to be. So, if you like, save all that firm commitment for the big fights. Just be clear that you are doing what *you* want to do and not just turning your back on something because you don't want to bother.

If your dog is indeed a nice dog with no problems of aggression or disobedience, you might just leave him in the kitchen, let him sleep on the couch or cover the couch with a pretty, washable throw. I've seen awfully sane people go all these routes. However, if you want to stop the problem, you must correct the dog each time he goes up on the furniture, whether you catch him in the act or just find telltale clues. Of course, you can strengthen your position by use of the Serendipitous Method. While you prevent and correct, also teach your dog GO TO YOUR PLACE. Prepare a warm and cozy corner for him and teach him, by taking him there at first on leash, to go there when told. Praise him for doing so. Praise him when he begins, on his own, to retire to his fluffy towel or pillow. This might be the final key to stopping him from resting on your favorite spot. Now he'll have one of his own.

The question I am always asked is whether or not you can have your cake and eat it too. Can the dog go up on one chair and not all the furniture? Of course he can. Tell him GOOD BOY, pat the chair that's his and invite him up. When he hops up on anything else, be indignant and tell him NOOOOO, OFF. Simple. Just be consistent. You also can have your cake and eat it when it comes to sharing not only board but bed with your dog, but there are other complications involved when bed is the issue.

Dogs in Bed

I guess I never *really* outgrew my teddy bear. I must confess that there are times when I love nothing better than a big, cuddly dog— in bed. It has to do with more than just cuddling. It can be a real problem. First, if you let the dog come into the bed at will—*his*—he will. He will do it clean or dirty, wet or dry, fleas, ticks, dirty toe- nails, with his raunchy bones and chew toys, during the shedding season (all year for my dog), etc. He will come up when you are alone and when you are not. It can be, at the very best, a mixed blessing.

Once entrenched, dogs do not like to be dispossessed from bed. If your dog has any vague notion of being aggressive, bed will bring it out. You roll over, he's in the way, it's hot, you can't sleep, you tell him OFF and he growls. It's three in the morning. It is dark. You are alone except for this growling dog. Who needs it?

Dogs are territorial. They are possessive. The bed, your bed, be- comes the dog's den. Now, to further complicate matters, the dog, a male, favors you. You begin by letting him on the bed when your husband is away overnight on business. When hubby returns, dog is supposed to sleep on the floor. So why is he growling at your husband? Why, when your husband gets out of bed in the morning, does the dog jump in and urinate on his side of the bed? Think it's funny? It happens.

The dog, great fun to warm your feet on during long, cold nights, is a real creature, not a teddy bear. So he gets feelings about sleeping up on the nice big bed, too, and feeling close to you and possessive over you, even protective. Why should he shove over or shove off to allow room for someone else? It's *his* place.

With all these caveats, there is a way, as promised, to have your cake and eat it, too. Just keep control. Let your dog up on the bed when *you* give permission. Pat the bed. Tell him OK. Tell him UP. You choose. If he puts paws or body up on the bed at any other time without being told he may—even if you want him in bed—tell him NO, SHAME, OFF. Teach him OFF or DOWN by using the leash and do it when you are not lying in bed. You should be able to send him back to the floor in the middle of the night without getting up or even fully waking up. He should neither object nor sneak back up after you fall back to sleep.

Your dog must understand that it is a privilege, not a right, to sleep on your bed. He must also learn that it is a privilege to sleep in your room. Since we can never predict all the eventualities of a lifetime, ours or the dog's, at least once a week have him sleep out of your room. You never know when you will want him out of your room or have to have him out. He should accept this without whining all night or urinating in the hallway. To avoid serious, bizarre, unnecessary confrontations, both these choices *must* belong to you, not your dog.

In fact, dogs do not always like to share what is theirs with uninvited (by them) strangers, and if they feel you are theirs, and your bed is theirs, you can be in real trouble. In this case, prevention is indeed what we are talking about, even if you think your sweet pussycat would never growl at anyone. It's not only assertive breeds that can be a problem if they form the habit of sleeping in your bed. A lot of the trouble comes from feelings of possessiveness, something all dogs are subject to, big and little. One of the worst bedroom fiends I ever met was a nasty Lhasa who had, for some strange reason, been part of a custody suit in a divorce case. The wife won the dog, who came complete with a few winning habits. He'd let her new beau into bed. But when the poor fellow wanted to get out, the dog, who hid under the bed, would dart partway out and bite his feet as he tried to make his getaway. There are not very many men around who are flexible enough for that kind of treatment!

Even if you remain celibate, your dog will have to sleep away from you sometime. You may go on vacation, get ill, visit fussy friends. It is best to raise him to be a bit more casual about where he sleeps so that the options remain in your hands. He will accept any way you raise him. He will not sulk, unless you spoil him first and then take away his rights later. Even then, he'll eventually adjust. But prevention is not that hard. Enjoy your cake.

Speaking of cake, what about dogs in bed with your little cookies? Is it okay for kids and dogs to share bed, toys, p.j.'s and night-lights? Should you worry about—yeech—dog germs, diseases, fleas on your children? With some common sense and a lot of heart, you can come to a fast, terrific answer. Follow the same precautions above— banish the beast once a week—but otherwise it is perfectly fine. If they can't sleep with kids, what on earth are dogs for, anyway?

6

Problems of Aggression

One cloud is sufficient to eclipse a whole sun.
—Baltasar Gracian, *The Oracle*

Dealing Effectively With Canine Aggression

If your dog growls at you when you are playing tug of war and at no other time, you don't have an aggression problem. If he growls at you or your children when he's eating, when you give him a command, when you try to put a collar or a leash on him, you do have a problem. If he just nips and he's young, the prognosis is good. If he bites, if he menaces you or frightens you in any way and he's no longer a puppy, you do have a serious problem which will not go away on its own. With work, it may be solved. It may have no cure at all. That depends on the age of your dog, how assertive he is, how assertive you are or can train yourself to be, how long the problem has existed and, no doubt, how lucky we three are—you, he and I.

Aggression from a dog toward his own master seems to rank as almost too heinous a crime to discuss. It is, to most people, the ultimate betrayal: the dog who bites the hand that feeds him. But that shocked attitude is an unrealistic way to look at dogs. If you want gratitude and hand-kissing, don't buy a dog. Creatures act in accordance with their natures, not with books of rules nor artificial morality. Your dog has neither the capacity nor the desire to sit around recounting all the good things you've done for him. If he's biting you, he may be thrown together of poor genetic fabric. He may be too aggressive, trigger-happy, touchy or fearful. He may feel a need to defend himself against imaginary enemies—even you. Perhaps you've laid down no rules. He may bite because he's spoiled rotten and for weeks or months or years he has been able to walk all over you. Perhaps, because he's a dog and you're a person, you never even knew he was doing it or testing you. You thought he was just a dog and that's the way dogs are: you can't touch them when they are eating, you can't control them when they see other dogs, you can't stop them from marking in the house once in a while, you can't really keep them off the furniture. Perhaps you thought he was too dumb to train. Perhaps, all along, he was grooming himself for the presidency and you just didn't notice.

Biting is the hardest dog problem to correct and the most serious to leave uncorrected. A biting dog, even a small one, is a formidable adversary. He is a menace to you and your family because he may bite any time he feels crossed. He is a menace to the whole neighborhood because, as careful as you are, he may get out loose one day by mistake. If your dog has just started to growl or bite, he may not be too difficult to retrain, but any dog that's been biting for more than a few weeks will tend to get more aggressive before he gives it up. If this is the awful truth at your house, please do some serious soul searching before you do anything else. Think about the risks involved in attempting to retrain your dog. Think also about the ultimate result. Either you will successfully stop your dog's aggressive behavior or you will have to put the dog to sleep. If you begin and then stop while there's still a biting problem, you will have inadvertently trained your dog to be a much stronger, more confident adversary. There is hope, yet this is not a problem to be taken lightly. You may decide to obtain help from a professional dog trainer and not go it alone.

Prevention and Correction: The Rules Are the Same

Biting can almost always be prevented by the use of common and a little uncommon sense in dog rearing. The following seven important steps may prevent you from having to correct a full-blown aggression problem when your dog is all grown up. All seven are also your guidelines for working with adult aggressive dogs.

STEP ONE: *Always be the winner.* If you give your dog a command, he *must* obey it. If you are too tired or too busy or don't know how to enforce the command, do not give it in the first place. If you give commands and do not make your dog obey, he will get progressively more and more disobedient. As he learns that he can walk all over you, he will eventually get the idea that he can run things altogether—and far better than you can. He will begin to compete for pack leadership. At this point, his aggressive behavior will be strongly motivated. However, if you show him early on that you are a firm and serious leader, he will never take that path.

STEP TWO: *Correct all signs of aggression.* You'd be surprised at the number of nice people who call up dog trainers for help with biting dogs and then cover up for their dogs. If owners, desperate for help, lie to dog trainers, what chance is there that they tell themselves the truth, even in the privacy of their own secret thoughts. Daydreams seem to persist, sometimes even through several episodes of tetanus shots and stitches.

If owners can't stand to think about biting, what distortions do you think occur with lesser crimes, symptomatic of dreadful things to come. How many excuses can a person invent for a nip, a growl, a scratch, a bared tooth or even just cheeky behavior? Before you read on and waste your precious time, ask yourself if *you* are ready to see what's there and call it by its rightful name. If not, close the book, take your lumps and bites, tell your lies and, when the abuse gets more than you can stand, put the dog to sleep.

Your dog is a pack animal. He's built to try to get away with anything he can. If you've got a cold, he'll take advantage of you—just as your kids will. If you pretend he's just playing, he's just fooling, he's just clearing his throat, he's just this or just that, he'll be on his way. Correct it all. Nipping is normal in a puppy. Correct it. Defecating on the rug is normal, too, and you correct that, don't you? He must learn never to put teeth on you, never to growl at you, never to disobey. Never. He will remember, not like a dog, but like an elephant, all the excuses you make for him, and he'll pay you not in gratitude but in spades. He's not mean. He's not an ingrate. He's just a dog.

He must learn, at your knee, just as he began to at his mother's, not to bite, not to growl—not to be a smart-mouth, fresh canine. He can be happy respecting you as alpha dog. You cannot be happy—or safe—if he takes on that role. So correct each and every sign of aggression.

STEP THREE: *Correct and praise appropriately.* Inappropriate praise is a common encourager of aggression. A friend or friendly stranger approaches. Your dog growls or even takes a hackles-raised aggressive stance and shows his dental work. You, to calm him, pet him, hug him, speak softly to him. "There, there," you mutter. You have just praised your dog for inappropriate aggression. You didn't mean to. You're not a bad person. It just happens that your misunderstanding of how the dog interprets your behavior caused you to do the opposite of what you should have done. The message your dog got, loud and clear, was therefore exactly the opposite of the one you wished to send.

The dog will interpret your correction or your praise as follows: (1) It applies to the most recent thing he did. (2) If it feels good, you are happy, he is happy and he'll repeat that most recent behavior. If it feels bad, is scary or shows your marked displeasure, you are unhappy, he is unhappy and he'll *try* not to repeat that most recent behavior.

So if your dog growls at someone who is clearly not threatening you and you pet him to calm him down, you have just praised your dog for growling at friends and he will continue to do so. Any behavior you don't like must be followed immediately, the swifter the better (remember his mother), by a correction. This will let the dog know that you don't like what he did and that you will cause him displeasure when he does it. That is part and parcel of your privilege as alpha dog. (Figure out the reverse for yourself!) But how much to punish or correct? My guideline is so foolproof it's amazing. *Use the mildest correction that works.* This way, you are in no danger of overcorrecting—and in no danger of undercorrecting, at least not for long.

Let's take an imaginary dog, Herbert, for a walk. Herbert is strolling along, sniffing, marking, being curious, acting like a normal male. Someone comes from the other direction, a friendly stranger, and wishes to pet Herbert. You are not afraid. But Herbert decides you are in imminent danger and growls. Tell him NOOOO. He growls again. The first correction, a mild one, a logical first try, did not work. Therefore, you will need to use one that is stronger to get the point across, to always be the winner. Now, saying NOOO again, jerk the leash hard so that Herbert gets a collar correction. Now Herbert turns and looks at you. He tentatively wags his tail. He got the point. The stranger, unless he's a complete fool, has taken off down the block. You will have to watch Herbert's reactions in similar situations to see if this syndrome is over (highly doubtful after only one good correction) or if it still needs more work (likely). After a time, with effective corrections, just what's needed and no more, the habit should stop. Perhaps, in this case, Herbert really had no idea that he shouldn't growl at everyone who came near you. Now you have begun to let him know. If you didn't, or if you petted him to calm him and let him know that everything was okay, he'd think, "Boy, did *I* do a good job. I chased that bad person off. Wow, am I tough. My master is happy. He's petting me and talking sweetly." And soon Herbert would be on his way to the pound.

Suppose the stranger, for his own demented reasons, did not take off. Then, after the second correction, Herbert is standing there wagging his tail and he allows the stranger to pet him. *Now* praise him so that he will, in the future, understand that *this* is how you expect your dog to behave, that *this* is what pleases you. He will be motivated to repeat this easygoing behavior and be less *over*protective, though not necessarily less protective.

Appropriate praise is just as important as appropriate correction. Many owners get so involved in correction that they forget to praise. In fact, one of the secrets of good dog training, that which separates the professionals from the amateurs, is not a knack for making firm corrections. Really, anyone can learn to do that. It is, instead, a special, warm, possessive and confident way of praising a dog that makes him want to give you the moon. Professional trainers handle the dogs they train as if they own them, as if they have the right to teach them, as if they were top dog. They make the dog feel good all over. They do not handle him tentatively, showing fear or discomfort. When he leans into them and looks up at their eyes, he sees self-confidence and love. When dealing with dogs, it's hard to have one without the other.

A good dog trainer will not replace nor augment praise with a food reward. While this is fine for teaching non-pack animals, dogs respond better and learn more deeply when there is no food around and when positive reinforcement is based on pack position and physical contact. Verbal rewards work well because they cause the same kind of pleasure response in the dog as petting and because dogs communicate verbally with each other. That is, they use a variety of sounds that have meaning.

Food rewards are fine for beginning trick work and as an acceptable shortcut with barking problems. However, when life-or-death obedience is the issue, food rewards should not be introduced. They hold the dog's attention rather than allowing it to be captured by the excitement of learning. Furthermore, if you do not have tidbits with you one day and your dog faces a genuine temptation, he is likely to ignore you. Rewarding a dog by petting and verbal praising are tools always available to you. They are valid, too, in that they integrate well with your dog's life as an animal and the way he communicates with, learns from and teaches others of his kind.

You can handle your dog and praise your dog the way a good professional trainer does, knowing you have the right and even the obligation to educate him properly. Only you can correct his unpleasant behavior and his dangerous behavior. Only you have the real obligation, pleasant though it may be, to hug your dog warmly for reactions and behavior you want repeated. Here is the true source of the bond between dog and man. It is not who puts down the chow who wins a dog's heart. It is the one who handles him firmly, consistently and affectionately.

STEP FOUR: *Teach him the basics and teach humanely.* Basic training gives you more than a wonderful repertoire of things a dog can do on command. It gives you and him a common language. It gives you control. It gives a dog a sense of security. Now he knows clearly what is expected of him and that he can deliver it. It helps ensure your position as pack leader. Training gives you the tools to readily remind your dog of his position in relation to you, thus reinforcing your alpha status. Anytime your dog acts up, tests, gets ornery or cheeky, you can use any command to get your point across: Me human, you dog.

Teaching is done via correction and praise. The voice is used for both positive and negative reinforcement. The leash is used with either a plain leather collar or a slip collar made of nylon or metal if you need one. Proper equipment will give you confidence and allow you to make rapid, kind and graceful corrections. Corrections can consist of voice commands alone, said firmly but never shouted, or leash corrections, which should always be "explained" by verbal commands or caveats which the dog knows. Occasionally, for acts of aggression or rampant destruction, you may want to imitate a dog correction by shaking your dog from side to side by his collar the way his mother gave him a shake or two when he was little and bad. As we will discuss later, some long-distance corrections also can be made, for special reasons, with water, using a plant mister, a water gun, a bucket or, in extremely dangerous cases, a hose. *Under no circumstances should you include hitting in your repertoire of corrections.* This warning refers to hitting a dog with your hand, or worse still, a rolled-up newspaper or his leash. Hitting is unnecessary, often ineffective and more likely to get you bitten than to stop the dog from biting. More often than not, hitting is a sign of our own ignorance, frustration and lack of patience.

STEP FIVE: *Let him earn his freedom.* Many people make the mistake of giving a dog too much freedom too soon. Often, they simply identify with the dog and feel that they would be miserable crated or locked in the kitchen all day, forgetting that the dog is not human and does not think with a human brain. He is, for one thing, a den animal, so that confinement for him has some plusses as well as the minuses we tend to see and exaggerate. His den is his castle and will give him security and safety, as well as teaching him to be clean in your home and not to chew up your furniture. The only sane way to raise a dog, for your sake as well as his, is to confine him when you bring him home and let him earn his freedom, as an appropriate reward for learning the behavior necessary to make him a good member of a human household.

Too much freedom, not too much loving, spoils. You can pet him as much as you like. You can kiss him all day long. You can feed him tidbits from your dish, buy him knucklebones at the butcher, shower him with rawhide chips and not spoil him one bit. However, if you give him run of the house before he's housebroken or let him be free to disobey, free to climb about on all the furniture, free to chew on your things, free to do as he likes when you like otherwise, you'll have a spoiled dog. A spoiled dog, all too often, becomes a biting dog. He wants his way. If you cross him, he will still try to get it—somehow. Biting may be his last resort, yet he may get to it. If begging fails, if convenient deafness fails, if sneakiness fails, if disobedience fails, if nipping, growling and running off to where you cannot retrieve him all fail, he may bite to get his way. Somewhere inside him, he knows it's a foolproof method.

Let him work for his freedom, piece by piece. The run of the house comes once he's housebroken and chew-proofed. Off-leash excursions come when he's reliable enough in his training, when he will come when called—each time, always. Freedom to join you in the dining room assumes he will not beg and freedom to join you on the bed assumes that he will leave without argument if you should decide against his company. When he can behave in the car, he can accompany you anywhere. When he has proven his manners, etiquette and civility, he can have all the freedom his master and his own intelligence will allow. To give too much too soon is asking for trouble.

STEP SIX: *Use the long DOWN, STAY, an owner's second-best friend.* During his training, your dog learns more than what SIT, DOWN, STAY, COME and HEEL mean. He learns that he must do *what* you want him to, *when* you tell him to, *where* you tell him to and *for as long as you wish.* The DOWN, STAY is the only sensible way to show the dog that a command must be executed for as long as you wish. Many dogs who appear to be well versed in the basic commands do not appear trained to the trained eye. This is because, although they may leap to a DOWN at even just a hand signal, they are humoring humans. They obey, as a trick, and bide their time until they are bored or impelled to do something else, in which case they simply break and go about their business. I have discovered, over the years, that most owners are so thrilled with the initial obedience that they totally ignore the importance of *the length of time* the command is carried out and the vital importance of the release. Many will cover for their dogs, doubly ensuring spoiling them, by breaking the dog a split second *after* he himself begins to break. For shame! Whom are you fooling? You certainly are not fooling your dog. He knows he started to get up before you quickly mumbled OK.

The long down, and by long I mean at least half an hour, should be pushed at the end of all the basic commands. This is the time, once you've gotten through on the other points, to let your dog know that timing is indeed on your side and in your capable hands. Place the dog on a down, check your watch and plan for a fifteen-minute stay. Each and every time he breaks, say NO and place him back in the same spot—exactly the same spot. He must not win an inch or a minute. If he truly understands that he cannot rise without a release from you—a mighty important level so far untouched in his previous training—he may well fall asleep. This is fine. There's no particular point in staying awake. Falling asleep on a down is actually a sign that your dog accepts training and clearly understands that he cannot get up until he hears a release word from you. When he wakes up or when you wake him and say OK, he will remember that he was there on command. Do not, however, put him on a DOWN, STAY and leave the room or go away. In that case, he will eventually awaken and, finding himself alone and abandoned, will break the command himself. This is not what you want him to feel he can do. Some folks, to keep a dog off the bed, put him on a DOWN, STAY and go to sleep. They are surprised to find the dog in bed with them in the morning. I, on the other hand, would be surprised to find him, under those circumstances, on the floor.

Decide on a length of time—fifteen minutes, five minutes, three minutes, twenty minutes—for that day's practice. Naturally, you can do a few brief DOWN, STAYS, too—but do not change your mind and make a twenty-minute one a five-minute one because you know your dog is going to break. The whole point now is to push. This sort of pushing will put him on a new and deeper level of obedience. He will really look to you. He will stop humoring you. You'd be surprised how well trained a poorly trained dog can look. Once a dog can do a half-hour DOWN, STAY, he will work more smoothly and with much more patience than ever before, and this work will improve, as if by magic, all his other training.

You can use the long, long down when you are stuck at the vet's for an hour, when you take your dog visiting or shopping, when your dog is acting the fool and you just would like to read quietly, when you are busy and he is pestering to go out or play. You can cool his heels with the long down. You can sometimes get through to an aggressive dog. You can often calm a fearful dog. You can increase the self-confidence of a shy dog by making him stay instead of letting him bolt. All this can be accomplished with the long, long down. So, practice. Your dog will never get to Carnegie Hall if you don't.

STEP SEVEN: *Limit roughhousing.* Rough play can be fun for both dogs and owners. However, it is a poor idea if your dog is aggressive, since it encourages biting, tugging, growling, nipping and wildness—all the things we want to prevent or stop. Rough play can be replaced by active play—running, jumping, retrieving, swimming. Play with your aggressive dog should not include push-away games, playing roughly on the floor, allowing the dog to pull on clothes,

permitting him to bite on your hands or bite on your arm or swinging the dog up in the air as he holds onto something with his teeth.
When you play with your dog, play it smart.

The Fear Biter vs. the Aggressive Dog

It is not as simple as you might imagine to tell a fear biter from
an aggressive biter for sure. When you are in the throes of a confrontation, you won't have time for a long, sit-down analysis. A
shortcut, as speedy yet as accurate as possible, is in order.

The aggressive dog is of one mind. He is confident, trigger-happy
and full to the brim with dog-style macho. He is go, go, go. He is on
his toes, hackles raised, ears forward, tail up, eyes looking at you. In
short, everything is forward, toward his intended victim. He may be
pleasant one moment and furious the next. When he is angry, there
are no holds barred. He lets it all hang out. In that, he is, at least
once he gets his dander up, more predictable than the fearful dog.

The fear biter, or shy-sharp dog, is ambivalent. His body language
will reflect that. His hackles may be up but his ears may be back. He
may come at you, yet keep his tail tucked under. His message is
clear: "I am unclear." He bites in imaginary self-defense, being triggered by a touch, a noise, a fast movement, a threat or supposed
threat. He is unpredictable and may bite even when not crossed or
not actually in danger. Often, poor breeding followed by poor socialization produces such a dog and the prognosis, though not entirely
grim, is not terrific either. Even if you socialize him painstakingly
and build his confidence, even if you correct his aggression and
teach him the basics, he may always be a fearful animal and may always have an unpredictable biting problem.

Like the fearful dog, the goosey dog is a nervous animal. He is the
dog who bites when you make contact with one spot, or two, on his
body. He is extremely sensitive and excruciatingly ticklish. He can
be an acceptable pet when handled with care, but this means
explaining to all guests and to all people he comes into contact with,
that he can only be handled in certain ways. One goosey dog I
worked with had ticklish hips, a very common area for this problem.
He nailed four people, all of whom made the tragic error, after petting his head and seeing a wagging tail, of petting down his sides.
Now who could guess that you couldn't pet the body of a friendly
dog? Careful handling and gradual desensitizing may make the

goosey dog a safer pet. Obedience training is a must. Caution, unfortunately, is the byword.

Correcting the Aggressive Dog— Starting From Scratch

NIPPING: If you have a puppy or an adult dog and he nips you, you should make him stop. (Stop laughing. I *am* going to tell you how.) A nip is a little bite that usually does not break the skin and is delivered when the dog is excited, often at play. It is a normal way for a dog to play with other dogs and even with people. However, since it is an undesirable habit to exercise on people, *it* should be nipped in the bud.

If your dog is very small or very young, grasp his collar to stop his wildness and tell him NO. If he continues to nip, flick him under his chin by snapping your forefinger off your thumb, assertively and seriously saying NO, NO as you do this. If your dog is over six months old and won't stop nipping after the above corrections, grasp his collar (all dogs should wear collars when loose with owners so that corrections can be made if necessary) and shake the dog back and forth three or four times. The shake, reminiscent of his mother's swift and fair justice, is a powerful yet extremely humane correction for a serious offense. When you shake a dog, his back feet should remain planted on the floor and his front legs move a foot or so to the left, the right, the left and the right again. Each shake is accompanied by NO! This is not to be used for minor offenses. Save it for the biggies. Using a leash for the corrective shake is excellent and easy and keeps you absolutely safe from the dog who gets more aggressive before he gets less so. Unless he is too big for you, and this is entirely individual, you can hold him off, if need be, via the leash. If he is bigger than your arm's length and doing more than nipping, you should get professional help.

If the shake, done once or twice, doesn't stop the nipping, at least for the moment, confine the dog away from all people, fun and activity. Grumble as you do so. Let him know that with *his* manners, all he's good for is the bathroom, laundry room, basement or crate. Let him cool off. Later, play with him again and see if he's absorbed anything. As you work, the nipping should stop more easily, eventually on just a NO.

GROWLING: If your dog growls at you, it's more serious than a nip. He's not just using his mouth in play. Now he's finding out if he can back you down, scare you off and run the show. You mustn't let him. If you're scared (we're not pulling any punches here, remember?) or feel he's too big to handle (over seventy-five pounds gets iffy for most owners) or if you don't feel you can handle him assertively, call in professional help, call in a tough friend, call in the Marines—but *do something*. If your growling dog is backing you down, he is getting more aggressive and more self-confident by the day. Act immediately or you will have to put the dog to sleep.

If you can handle him yourself, you must win at each session. This means that you get to growl last. Even if you go clear through the night, the last sound heard must come from your throat, not his. If you correct him and he rattles ever so slightly in his throat, in his eyes, he's won—and when he wins, you lose. When you lose, eventually he loses—permanently—so shut off the radio and television and even close the windows if need be; you must be able to hear him.

When working with an aggressive dog, have him on leash. A leather one is best so that you can handle it without hurting your hand. Also, keep a plant mister handy, filled with water laced with two or three tablespoons of white vinegar, as recommended in Chapter 4. If it makes you feel secure, you also can have a pot of cold water handy to toss in his face. It's fantastic for an element of surprise with many dogs and won't harm the dog. Of course, don't do it on the rug. But even though you'll have to mop it up from the kitchen or den floor, that beats patching up a dog bite.

Now, you can trigger the growl (you know what makes it happen) and be ready to correct the dog. Put down the food dish. Have Killer on leash, water standing by, bandages handy. Reach, carefully, for the dish. He growls. Jerk the leash as hard as you can, tossing him back and forth, back and forth, saying NO, NO, NO. If, when he is back on all fours, he is silent, tell him GOOD BOY and let him eat. That's it for the day. You've earned your points. Go sit down and shake in another room where he can't see you.

With a growler, you'll have to be prepared, as well, to be able to work when he growls and you didn't expect it or set it up. This may require plant misters to be stationed wherever doggy goes and it may even require you to have a leash trailing from your dog whenever you are home. If so, don't leave him alone with a leash on. He could

get caught and strangle or eat the leash and suffer dire consequences.

Now, when he growls because you called him to come or you
reached for his collar or you walked too near him or you touched
him where he's goosey, grab the end of the leash and make your correction. If he continues, try a few shots in the muzzle with the water
and vinegar. If he still continues, shake again, spray again and isolate
him.

BITING: Few owners can bail themselves out of this situation
alone. If your dog has become a full-blown biter, meaning he has
broken the skin with his teeth, has done so on several occasions, has
possibly forced someone to have medical care for a bite and is making you and others afraid, you will probably need professional help.
Shop around carefully to get a trainer who has been enthusiastically
recommended by someone you trust, by your vet or by the local kennel club. The first priority from now on is that no one else get bitten. This means that the dog may need some harsh handling; the
trainer must know precisely when to push forward and when to call
it quits for the day.

When working with a biting dog, timing is both important and
difficult. Even experienced trainers cannot be one hundred percent
accurate in handling the difficult dog or in predicting the final out-
come of training. I never guarantee that a biter will stop entirely. To
do so, I feel, would be a dangerous lie. I try my best. I work carefully and very hard. I hope for luck along the way. I also understand,
and explain to the dog's owner, that once a dog has crossed that in-
visible line, once he has overcome his strong inhibition against sink-
ing teeth into human flesh, he is more apt to do it again than a dog
who has never bitten. Through training, you will surely understand
him better, know how to handle him better, understand more about
how his aggression gets reinforced and how to counteract this, and
you may even stop him from aggressive acts entirely. However, it
will take a long time to be sure of that—years and years. No one can
pat himself on the back two or three weeks after beginning work
with a difficult, nasty dog and say the job is done and permanent.
Some dogs are worth the risk. If you work hard and use caution, too,
they may be a little touchy in situations you can control, but worth
keeping as pets anyway. However, I have seen some and worked
with some that had been biting for too long, were too crazy or too

nervous or just were too aggressive. Keeping a dog like that would be a persistent danger to the family or outsiders or both. I do not believe that it is worth keeping a dog alive at all costs. Some dogs are biters because of awful breeding practices and all the proper training and upbringing in the world would not change that fact one iota. Part of the advantage of seeking professional help is that you may get an honest, objective opinion. That alone can help you to be level-headed about a difficult, highly emotional matter.

I personally do not believe in mutilating dogs in the attempt to stop aggression. If training could not help reform an entrenched biter, I would not have his canine teeth removed nor have him altered. Some people feel that with the threat of a painful bite no longer an issue, they can settle down and train their pet without fear. Others feel that castration will tone down a male and make him less aggressive. This is true only when the dog is castrated when young and/or newly aggressive. Altering a male will have little or no effect on aggressive behavior that has been evident for three or four months or more. Furthermore, dog problems usually come in groups. Surgery will not change whole sets of bad habits nor alter the character of a bad-news dog. I have seen semi-toothless, castrated small dogs *continue* to terrorize their families, just as if nothing had happened. I would prefer to give a dog either a dignified life or a dignified death.

When attempting to retrain a biting dog, basic training, always on leash, should be reinforced and tightened up first. All corrections in training and for aggression must end with you the winner. You must emphasize your control over the dog yet praise good behavior whenever you have the opportunity to do so. Biting attempts should be corrected with a strong NO, NO, NO and a shaking, using collar and leash. If necessary, you should be able to hold the dog entirely off the ground by his collar and leash for your protection. He will not die from this harsh correction. Above all, he cannot bite you when he is off the ground. Moreover, he may eventually give up his aggression because your ability to "hang" him will show him clearly who the tougher dog is. This is a last resort and is not to be used lightly, nor on puppies or very small dogs, but if you are to work safely with a biter, you must be able to get him off the ground in an emergency. It is preferable to hitting, being clearer as a retraining technique and safer for you as trainer. Because it looks harsher than it actually is, it will deeply offend other people and should not be used, if possible, on a crowded street. In any case, most aggression toward owners, like most accidents, happens right at home.

You can use water laced with vinegar as a correction for aggression, too. Try, as well, to avoid certain situations that act as a red flag for your dog and trigger his aggression, unless these situations are just part of normal living and cannot be avoided. If so, then try to stop the biting for a reasonable amount of time—about two or three months. If there is no visible progress then, think again about keeping the dog as your pet.

A crate—for isolation after correction, for cooling his heels and for keeping him away from you while you cool your temper—is a superb idea.

Do not keep your aggressive dog tied up inside or out, as that tends to make a dog more aggressive. The constant frustration of pulling at the end of a rope makes a dog angry and sometimes just plain mean. A pen, a fenced yard, confinement to a crate (temporarily) or a small room are all preferable to tying a dog to an overhead line or an in-ground post. Keeping him away from people also exaggerates the problem. He must be and remain socialized. Obviously this is a true dilemma if he is a biter. All work must be done with extreme care.

Sex and Aggression: It's a Dog's Life

Having or not having a sex life will affect your dog. However, a dog will not be effected by his sex life or lack of it in the same way a person would.

A female dog will often be exactly the same after she raises her litter as she was before experiencing motherhood. While protecting a litter, even the gentlest bitch may bite. Once the puppies are weaned, she will be no more aggressive nor difficult to handle than she was before mating. A sex life will neither resolve nor create personality problems in female dogs.

The male will not be changed by fatherhood; he will be affected by his brief but stunning brush with his own sexuality. The impact this experience has on many males can be long-lasting and may not be something you desire in a pet. No more will he be Mr. Nice Guy. Mating turns most males very macho. The innocent male dog gets stirred up by the scent of a female in season. He may feel agitated or want to break out and roam, getting nearer to the pleasant odor that makes his blood rush so. Once bred, he will vie with other males for the right to mate and he will bully males and females alike, any chance he gets. Life becomes an arena where only the best male gets the female. Suddenly, genetic programming, passed along from generation to generation of pet dogs, reads: Wolf. *Déjà vu*, anyone? All females must be checked out. All males now look like competition. All bushes must be marked, just in case. He may be, from now on, less tractable as a pet and more aggressive with other *dogs*. He will not be more aggressive, or aggressive at all, toward *humans*, because of having been mated, unless he already was before. Of course, if he is aggressive toward people, he never should be bred. This is true, too, of the bitch. The chance that a trigger-happy mom or dad will spawn trigger-happy kids is far too great.

SOME TRICKS YOUR MOTHER NEVER TAUGHT YOU

1. *Aggression toward other dogs and how to avoid dogfights*: Most dogfights happen because of carelessness. Your dog does not *have* to like or play with every dog he sees. If you watch him and get to understand his behavior patterns, dogfights and aggression toward other dogs can almost always be avoided. Most areas have leash laws. If your dog is leashed and growls at another dog or raises his hackles, first correct his unnecessary aggressive display with a firm leash correction and a no-nonsense NO. Then promptly remove him from the proximity of the other dog. If you ask for and get agreement from the owner of the other dog, you can, instead, stay long enough to make two or three corrections. Always follow up with praise when and if the dog acts blasé toward the other dog after your correction.

Sometimes the leash, your instrument of control and safety, can be the *cause* of aggressive feelings. On leash, your dog feels more confident. The control the leash offers makes him feel more frustrated as well as more feisty. Like the held-back drunk who says, "Let me go and I'll rip him to pieces," so the leashed dog feels tougher when held than when free. However, good judgment must be exercised before dogs are set free in the hope that they will play.

Sometimes, when free and given room to maneuver, dogs will work things out on their own in a peaceful fashion. They will sniff each other out, be a bit pushy, growl, walk on their toes and then play like puppies—but not always. Males often take an instant dislike to other males, particularly but not only if they have been bred or if there is a bitch around, even a spayed one. Some males, depending on breed, temperament, environment, training and perhaps their hormones, take to easygoing play with other male dogs more or less all the time. Others never do. Bitches are less likely to fight—yet they may. You must know *your* dog and watch the other dogs. If everyone seems amenable and your dog will come back when called, you can let him play in the park with the other dogs— but don't do so with eyes closed. A feisty male may turn up after you make your initial decision. A bitch may arrive and change the chemistry of the group. So it is your job to avoid trouble by monitoring the dogs while they play.

If, with all your care and attention, a fight breaks out, try to break it up without getting your hands in it. Any way you can douse the dogs with water often works to shock them enough to get them apart. If the dogs have tails, a person pulling each dog away from the other by the tail can be effective. Some people grasp the hind legs of both dogs and lift them off the ground, but a dog in the middle of a fight may just lash out and bite, even if he would not normally do so. In the confusion of fighting, a dog may bite anything in his way—even you.

There is no magic way of breaking up a dogfight without getting hurt. If you are lucky enough to have a hose handy or a blanket to toss over the dogs' heads, use those things. However, you may have to decide, and rather quickly, if you will just stand by and let the dogs battle it out or if you are willing to plunge in to separate them with the knowledge that you will probably be bitten. Prevention looks more appealing by the minute.

2. *Aggression toward people in uniform:* Your nice dog may only dislike the mailman, the meter reader and, worse yet, policemen. He may dislike them with a passion, a passion you'd like to cool. Several factors influence his peculiar aggression toward people in uniform.

Your dog, an ordinary fellow, doesn't like anything out of the ordinary and he doesn't like change. Show him a person who looks a little different from the rest of us and you get his suspicious juices running. That's just part of being a dog. One day, you may come home sporting a new hat and your dog may not know you, for the moment, from a hole in the wall. He may even bark at you, just as if you were a stranger. How embarrassed he'll be to find out who you really are. But that's his problem.

Your dog has a more interesting investment in menacing people in uniform. His initial dislike of them may come from the fact that they approach your house, with the mail or the meter cards or the package you ordered. Your dog barks, mildly exercising his instinct to protect his property. What happens then? They retreat. He doesn't know that they retreat because they have finished their job, that they would retreat even if he never opened his big yap. He assumes that *he* chased them off.

Each time your postal person delivers the mail, he or she delivers as well, free of charge, an agitation session in which the dog wins and becomes more secure as an aggressor. Every time the meter reader leaves to the tune of your dog's excited barking, the dog grows more hair on his chest. In order to stop this accidental vicious circle, you must step in.

Your agitators, in this case, are working for you gratis and unbeknownst to them. Fine. There's not much that's free nowadays. Five minutes before the mail comes, or when you see the meter reader down the block, leash your dog, drop the leash and go about your business. When your dog starts climbing the walls and the front door and working himself up to chomp on any uniformed leg he could get his teeth on, grab the leash, jerk back hard and tell him ENOUGH. NO would make him think he should never bark at the door—and, of course, sometimes he should. He shouldn't do it *ad nauseum*, though, and he should, under any circumstances, stop when you tell him to. Use a firm voice and the leash correction as many times as you need to, putting your dog on a SIT, STAY as soon as you can to help calm him down. In this way, you will communicate to your dog that you do not consider the postman a threat and he need not get quite so hot under the collar. He had no idea you disapproved before. In fact, from his splendid results, he probably assumed it was the best thing he had going for him. It is now up to you, by patient monitoring and repetition, to change his mind.

3. *A biting dog under the bed*: Buy a flat leather collar for your dog. Attach a nylon cord, the weight of which reflects the size of your dog. Do not use a clothes line on a Chihuahua! Tie the cord to the collar. Put the collar on the dog. Help the dog to want to hide under the bed and menace you by getting into bed, out of bed or whatever is necessary to trigger the action. Safely ensconced in his den, he can now play the tiger and rule the house with his iron jaws. Right? Wrong!

Call him sweetly. If he does not come out immediately or if he hangs back and growls or snarls, pick up the end of the rope (which you cleverly made a couple of feet longer than the width of your bed and which you cleverly knotted at the end for easier handling) and yank, hard. If your dog bumps his head on the way out, so much the better, as long as you moderate the yank to his size, as usual. Have him sit front, as if he came all by his good little self, and praise him for coming. Drop the cord or string. See what happens. If it's a repeat, you repeat. He must learn, before he wanders around with no strings attached, that you have the power to control him, even to get him out from under the bed. He may or may not understand how—all the better if he doesn't.

4. *Catch me if you can:* Many dogs like to snatch objects to gain attention. They race around, trying to entice you to follow and, if at all possible, to become frantic. It is part of their very special and uncanny talent that they learn to snatch the things that are most important to you. That helps ensure the desired chase game and creates more excitement than a barrel of cats.

If your dog plays catch-me-if-you-can with your cigarettes, you can either stop smoking or use the cord-on-collar correction. Now, when he taunts you from the other side of the dining room table, call him to come, gently pull the cord—*look*—dog and cigarettes. What if he growls over your Marlboros? You have the cord. Use it to shake him, saying NO, NO, NO, and then tell him OUT. If he doesn't drop the prize at your feet, do the shake correction again. If the second shake won't get your slightly wet and broken cigarettes back for you, pull up on the string until the front of your dog is in the air and tell him OUT. By now, you're mad enough to try this, even though he may weigh eighty or ninety pounds. When he drops the package, do not punish him. The punishment would seem to apply to the last thing he did—returning your cigarettes. Praise him, though not warmly, release him and light up.

5. *Growling over food and bones:* Some people wonder how to get food away from a dog who is growling while hovering over bowl or bone. One method is, of course, to leash the dog (this may mean *planning* the confrontation, which is okay) and jerk him away from the bowl, saying NO. Rather than lose, if the incident happened and the leash was not on the dog, I'd dump a pot of cold water on his head and dish and then, while still feeling victorious, use the incident as an excuse to clean my kitchen floor.

You might have to be creative and think quickly. Sometimes a sudden noise will distract a dog away from his food for just a moment. If you use it well, a moment may be all you need. Have someone ring the doorbell or call the dog from another room, or clap your hands over the dog's head. If he picks his head up to look, give bone or bowl a kick and send it flying. Once you extricate dog from food, grab his collar, snap on the leash and, in a very businesslike fashion, give a command. Out of habit and surprise, he will probably work—just as if nothing had happened. If you end up on top, he'll know that that's where you belong.

6. *Aggression toward children:* See Chapter 10, Transitions, and Chapter 14, Problems With Other People's Dogs.

FINAL OPTION CLAUSE

People like to think they have more options than they do when they fail to retrain an aggressive dog. The most unlovable monster can be lovable to his owner, so it can be painful beyond words to have to put a dog to sleep, even if he's bitten you. An owner's feelings for his pet are deep and genuine. Even when they are unrealistic and foolishly hopeful, feelings cannot be discounted. I have never taken a client's affection for his dog lightly, nor should you treat your own feelings that way.

However, if you have a dangerous dog and you have given his retraining your best shot and failed, you do not have the option of keeping him anyway. Neither can you give him away, sell him, pass him on to a breeder or even put him in the pound. If you tell the truth, no one else will want him. If he is unsafe for you, he will be unsafe for anyone else, in all but very rare cases. This being so, he should be painlessly put to sleep by your veterinarian. It is the only humane and honest thing to do. If that makes you sadder than almost anything you can think of, that is a fair and reasonable testimony to the fact that you loved your dog and tried your best.

When you finish crying, which may take hours or months, you may want and need another dog. That, too, will be a testimony to the love you felt for the dog you lost, and is just fine. No one honest ever promised you a life without tears, for if you had one, it would mean that you never took a chance and loved another creature, man or beast. And that's an option I'm sure you don't want.

7

Shyness, Nervousness, Hyperactivity and Fear

Can we understand at all, ever, where we do not love?
—Sherwood Anderson

Overcoming Shyness

Shyness is the kind of problem that causes a dog at least as much distress as his owner. If the light of your life steals a steak now and then, sits on your couch with muddy feet or hogs the bed, the only pain he'll feel is the pain you may inflict on him for stepping over the line. However, a shy dog, like a shy person, is in pain much of the time. He senses danger lurking everywhere. He fears shadows, quick movements, strangers. A sudden noise may send him fleeing to another room, bolting right out of his collar on a busy street or it may begin a gruesome half hour of nonstop shaking. He is often thinner than he should be, burning off calories by the hundreds when he is fearful, picking at his food, losing his appetite because a spoon drops a few feet away. He misses out on all the cooing, petting and friendships that most dogs thrive on, as well as the subsequent relaxation that this physical contact provides. He may hide when guests enter your home, or he may be fine in familiar territory, but unequipped to face the rigors of the street—passing traffic, kids on bikes, strangers walking by. Sometimes, he seems fine with people but will freak out at the sight of another dog or any other animal. His appearance is not one of confidence and canine self-esteem. He suffers when there is no cause. He slinks, bolts, hangs his belly close to the ground, tucks his tail. He is useless as a natural protector of home and hearth. He should not be bred—and, if the problem is neglected, he may, one day, bite in his imaginary need for self-defense.

A shyness problem may arise from insufficient socialization early in a dog's life. Perhaps, as a puppy, he was left with the litter too long. He may have been one of the more submissive dogs in the group and he may have been jumped on, terrorized or beaten too many times. The whole world, it may seem, is made up of enemies. He has no basis for feeling confident. In some cases, human contact was neglected for too long and the dog will be shy of people. He may have been sent to his new home too young and not have learned from his mother and his littermates how to fight for himself, how to toe the mark, how to stand up, when to back down. He has not learned how to find a place for himself that is comfortable, safe and appropriate. His shyness may be caused by poor breeding. Perhaps a nervous bitch was bred anyway for her great coat, good head or fabulous pedigree. He may be genetically programmed to be shy or he may even have learned to be fearful at his mother's knee.

In some cases, while breeding was sound and early socialization sufficient, once he was placed in his new home he was isolated from exposure to the world. He lives, perhaps, with one person who is rich enough to have a large, fenced yard; therefore, he never gets to go exploring, meet new people, face up to the challenges of modern life —machines, cars, noise, crowds. Unaccustomed to change, he learns to fear anything unfamiliar.

Shyness is also increased, at times, by a well-meaning owner who comforts a shy dog with tenderness, love and what he assumes to be understanding. He removes all causes for fear rather than aiding the dog to get used to what frightens him. Furthermore, when the dog does get frightened, he is reassured with soft words and petting. In the dog's eyes, he is getting praised for acting fearful. Thus, the problem gets compounded, even with the best of intentions.

It can be very helpful to have a detailed history of any dog with any problem. In this way, you may have one or several specifics to work with and help the dog overcome. Although a lack of information will make for more guesswork, any shy dog can be helped. Expectations should be realistic. One cannot count on turning a basket case into a social butterfly, nor even make a terribly shy dog suitable for breeding. But with reasonable goals, progress can be visible and highly satisfying, ensuring a far less painful existence for your pet and possibly overcoming the difficulty entirely.

While it is true that tender, loving care is important for a shy dog, love by itself is not the answer. Love and praise must come for positive actions on the part of the dog. The goal is then to determine when love is constructive and can help the dog.

An important first step in aiding a shy dog is to accustom him to a collar and leash. A leather collar is preferable, in this case, to a choke chain. Once used to the limitations he has while on leash, he will begin to gain confidence from the control and structure you will begin to provide. Your own confidence will travel down this umbilical cord right to the dog. Gradually, via use of the leash and training, you can help him to face up to the things that cause fear. He will learn to stand his ground in spite of his feelings of panic. Furthermore, he will be praised for doing so. Little by little, he'll learn that he *can* cope with a noisy child, a passing bus or a dropped dish —and that it's not that hard, after all. And he'll be earning your praise in the bargain. Not a bad deal.

A simple SIT, STAY is an essential tool for working with a shy dog. Once he can execute this command in the protected quiet of your living room, you can begin to teach him to face adversity by demanding that he hold his ground rather than fleeing.

THREE CASE HISTORIES

Cybil the Shepherd Gains Confidence

Cybil, a German Shepherd bitch, would run and hide when anyone came to her owner's front door. Making friends with her the first time took ages. This was accomplished with the use of the training leash and lots of patience and tenderness. A SIT, STAY with the leash in the hands of a stranger showed Cybil that she would not die sitting six feet away from someone she feared. Going beyond that first step on the first session might be impossible, depending on the degree of shyness the dog exhibits. A shy dog must be pushed slowly and never cornered or overwhelmed.

After a week of practice with her owner, Cybil became rather proud of her accomplishment and relished the praise for a job well done. On the second lesson, Cybil once again attempted to hide, but was brought back on leash and put on a SIT, STAY. This time I was able to pet her when it was time for praise. When she tried to bolt, she was corrected with NO, SIT, STAY and then petted very gently and verbally praised as well.

Eventually, we worked outdoors and taught Cybil to heel. While terrified of everything at first, she came to see that walking close to the side of the person holding the leash was a safe experience. Soon it became a pleasant experience. As training progressed and as Cybil progressed, her owner, at my request, invited some friends to lunch during a scheduled training session. We never forced Cybil to submit to handling too quickly. We did force her, via the SIT, STAY, to remain in the proximity of strangers, something she was unable to do before training. Eventually, a young girl from the neighborhood was hired to walk and work Cybil once or twice a week. She began to take her into the shopping area and even into stores, always correcting her expression of fear with a verbal correction and always insisting that she work. Cybil was loved and praised warmly for all new experience and was treated with patience, tenderness and a respect for her difficulties. By the termination of her training, Cybil was greeting people at the door, was comfortable on her walks and enjoyed the camaraderie of company, provided the group was small.

A Case of Kennel Shyness

Tuppence, a Field Setter, was bought at the age of six months after spending all her life in a kennel run, at first with her littermates and then by herself. Her owner was well aware of the difficulties this would cause and was willing to take her anyway. Housebreaking a kennel dog may present a serious problem, but, in this case, the owner took the sensible route and purchased a crate. Early adjustment to a home setting was mixed. Tuppence was superb with the family, including two young children, was confused about housebreaking and got severely carsick whenever she was taken for a ride, even if the duration was less than five minutes. She was ecstatic to meet strangers and showed no fear of animals. But when we began to teach her to heel and inevitably began to show her the world, her belly nearly scraped the ground. In her limited experience, she had never been exposed to traffic nor had she had the day-by-day exposure of learning to cope with the new and unfamiliar. She could get thrown by anything, and she did. We built confidence through training and gradual exposure, very limited in time at first. One must watch the animal closely in these circumstances and know when to push for a few more minutes and when the dog is going on overload. Our first visit to town was brief and we chose an area where cars and people passed, but not in great numbers. Eventually, Tuppence was able to test herself at the shopping center and hold her own with shopping carts, delivery trucks and even the fascinating innards of the five-and-ten. Her training and exposure should go on for quite a while, but the prognosis for her life as a well-balanced pet looks excellent.

Accidentally Encouraged Fear in a Shy Dog

Bruce, a Rough Collie, showed only the typical reserve of the breed when trained as a puppy. His owner, Mary, an eighty-two-year-old widow, was a retired teacher and lived rather quietly, but Bruce became the neighborhood mascot and not a day went by without some of the children coming to run him and play with him. He loved other dogs, was outgoing on walks and passed all the tests of training with flying colors. He even enjoyed a birthday party with the neighborhood kids when he reached the age of one. Shortly after that, months after his training, I received a distress call from his owner.

What had happened, it seemed, was that Bruce hung all his fears on one hook—the kitchen. He continued to be social with people and animals, continued to love his walks and an occasional excursion to the shopping street. However, if a sudden noise emanated from the kitchen, he'd run to the front door and, huddled in a corner, he'd tremble for a good fifteen minutes.

While questioning Bruce's owner about the details of the circumstances which caused him to run away and tremble and what her follow-up was, I learned that when Bruce became frightened, Mary got very upset and rushed to comfort him. Thus reinforced, his fear grew. We took Bruce into the kitchen and dropped a spoon; he took off. I found him huddled near the front door, shaking. Snapping on the leash, I took him back to the kitchen, put him on a SIT, STAY and let him sniff the offending spoon. At first, he tried to run, but I insisted on the stay. When he sniffed the spoon, I fussed over him and petted him. Then I dropped the spoon right in front of him.

When he broke and tried to escape, I firmly told him NO and made him sit and stay. Again, I let him sniff the spoon and I praised him warmly. He began to like the game.

We experimented with various kitchen noises, none of which his gentle owner made with any frequency. Mary said that Bruce would sometimes come in when she had dinner, but wouldn't come close enough to be touched and that he would run off at the slightest noise, like the sound her coffee cup made when she set it back on the saucer. I encouraged her to keep him in the kitchen, on leash, whenever she was there and to intentionally make noise with silverware and dishes, occasionally even dropping something onto the floor. We continued to work with Bruce, always preventing his escape and praising his new boldness. We began to clap for him the second the noise was made and, even though we felt a little silly, it was soon clear that all the cheering was having a fast, positive effect. Bruce lay down and soon we were able to toss the spoon to the floor behind his back and get a wagging tail instead of a disappearing act.

The key factors with Bruce were: (1) stopping praise for fear; (2) forcing him to hold his ground; and (3) praise for bravery. The big ham seemed more moved by applause than by fear. On a follow-up phone call, Mary reported that Bruce was voluntarily joining her for all her meals and clean-up chores. If he did occasionally bolt, Mary would get him, put him on leash and bring him back to the kitchen. He seemed very willing to stay the second time around.

In all three cases of shyness, the owners were committed, willing, patient and loving. None of the three considered giving up. All three followed suggestions and worked firmly but tenderly with the dogs. All three shy dogs progressed well enough so that they could be considered good pets and will be able to live out normal lives in loving homes. Even a dog of show quality with shy tendencies can be seasoned through training, appropriate praise, exposure and applause to take his place in history and stand up to the distractions, confusion and noise of the show ring. Many of the techniques used can easily be applied to other shy dogs to help them and their worried owners overcome a painful and difficult problem.

Your Shy or Fearful Dog

For your purposes, helping your own pet to overcome a painful problem, it doesn't really matter if you call the dog shy, fearful or nervous. Often these problems overlap and a dog that is simply shy and retiring can become a fear biter if mishandled. The line is too thin for us to get fussy about definitions.

Handling the dog and minimizing the problem are the important factors for us to deal with. Seasoning the dog is done with small doses of opposites. Feelings of security should be built in the dog, but never to the extent that he is in a silk-lined environment in which reality doesn't intrude its ugly head. The idea is to prepare the dog for any reality. So, while giving him a place of his own and time to himself, and treating him with love and understanding, he must, too, be handled firmly and taught to face the rigors of the real world.

He should not be protected from noise, though you won't want to overwhelm him with a day of lightning or sirens. Little by little, he should be exposed to whatever he fears and at the same time should be praised for moments of bravery, for standing his ground, for facing up. He should never, as the case histories illustrate, be praised when turning tail and trying to escape.

His seasoning should be planned, but flexible, always amended if he can progress more quickly or is showing signs of stress. One thing a professional trainer will do that pet owners seldom do without instruction is to plan ahead, knowing the goal and working out a reasonable schedule of how to get there and how long that will take. You can do that with your own fearful dog, planning short excursions at first, say three times a week. As you work, you may increase the duration of your walks or adventures and the hecticness of the location. Continue to do this as your dog gets increasingly able to handle activity, noise and crowds.

If your dog has a specific fear, it can be dealt with more easily than can a generalized fearful attitude. Some of the most common fears found in dogs are discussed individually below.

Fear of Stairs

Most puppies are afraid of steps, particularly backless stairs which permit you to see the ground below between each one. But they learn rather quickly in most cases to negotiate the climb up and down. If your puppy or grown dog is afraid of steps, put his leash and collar on him and walk him to the steps, talking briskly to him as you do. Your attitude, while attentive at all times, should be that this adventure will be fun. Success, even with great help from you, should always be rewarded warmly with verbal praise as well as petting.

The leash will give the dog all the confidence he needs. As you hold it, keep it quite tight so that the puppy or dog feels supported. That feeling will let him know that he cannot fall. Even if he cannot understand that fact intellectually, he will feel secure enough to try the steps. Talking him through the ordeal, try to get him to follow you up or down the steps. If he will not do it fairly soon after you begin to coax him, tug hard so that he is forced to do the first step. Holding the leash firmly so that he cannot slip or fall, praise him like mad for the one step and begin to coax again. You may have to tug for a few steps or even at a few sessions. Most dogs will rapidly do the whole flight once they see they can do a step or two with you going along at their side and the leash held high. Practice until your dog will negotiate the flight, both up and down, without the leash. Continue to praise and even make a game out of the trip for a few weeks, ensuring that the dog will stay pleased with this new skill. Another good trick while the dog is still unsure is to lift him and place him in the middle of the flight. Of course, you'll be there holding the leash to offer both moral and physical support for his trip.

With a little effort, you can save your dog a lot of agony and you can save yourself from continually carrying the dog when steps are in the way of where you and he must go.

Fear of Storms

Many dogs who are afraid of storms have picked up their fear from their owners. Whatever the cause, you can help the dog overcome it. However, if you are the one who passed this fear to your dog, you might not be the ideal trainer in this case. A matter-of-fact attitude, requiring the dog to hold his ground (the SIT, STAY is perfect here) and lots of reassuring praise for not running and hiding will be your winning ticket. Some books suggest playing tapes of thunder and teeming rain, but there are enough storms in one's lifetime for you to wait for and use the real McCoy, so you can let the poor dog breathe easily on sunny days. Besides, since animals are so much more in tune with nature and with all the atmospheric changes that go along with rain or snow or sunshine, it would really drive a dog to distraction for you to shuffle natural realities in the attempt to retrain him.

Fear of Children

Small dogs, nervous dogs, dogs that live with one or two adults and never see anyone shorter than five-one, sometimes act spooky around children. Children are noisier than adults, they move more rapidly and usually they are less predictable in their movements. They are more likely to step on a dog by accident and sometimes will even hurt a dog when they themselves have been punished.

It is always best to expose a dog to every possible eventuality when he is a puppy. Some careful breeders I know invite nice neighborhood kids to come and play with the puppies when the puppies are at the adorable, scampering stage. It is marvelous for both puppies and children.

It is, indeed, more difficult to expose a dog to children once he is afraid of them or doesn't much like them. Some dogs decide not to like kids because of a bad experience, just in the same way that kids sometimes will decide not to like dogs. Then the problem is where to find the kids to retrain the dog, who just might get upset enough to bite. Since this is quite tricky, the advice or aid of a professional might be a wise choice. If you continue to isolate the dog from children, he will get worse in relation to them. If you invite some poor, unsuspecting, rosy-cheeked youngster in for hot chocolate, he might go home in bandages.

A safe first step is to get the dog out. Kids are around, playing and riding bikes and dashing about. Get the dog used to that daily experience. If he shows any signs of nastiness, correct him with a hard tug on the leash and a firm NO. If he backs away, make him sit and stay and praise him when he has held his ground, but not while he is fleeing. Eventually, you will have to have him handled by youngsters. If he is not nasty and has not bitten, you can try with an older child who is not at all afraid of dogs. Do not hold the dog nor allow him to be cornered. You can have the child toss a ball or favorite toy for the dog to retrieve or let the child take the leash and walk the dog. Ideally, the dog should be inspired to go to the child on his own. Often a matter-of-fact attitude and a normal activity will help the dog change his mind.

As with any problem, do not expect miracles. Shy or fearful dogs are particularly slow to change. Their slowness is, in fact, part and parcel of a shyness problem.

Fear of Males or Females

Some dogs exhibit a fear of men or women—usually, people not of the same sex as their owner. This can result from the owner's own fears or from the dog's accidental lack of exposure early or even later in life. The problem can be alleviated by correcting the expression of fear or aggression and praising the dog for making friends with any member of the gender he fears. It will take the dog a few friendships before he begins to generalize. It is a good idea, as well, to have the dog worked and given commands by members of the gender he fears.

Fear of Racial Groups

Dogs who fear one or several racial groups are often picking up signals from their owners. A simple, matter-of-fact correction, NO, and a tug on the leash when aggression or fear is displayed will help. Have the dog handled gently by some individuals of the groups he fears. Praise the dog for standing his ground and behaving normally.

Fear of Random Objects

I have seen many dogs shy away from sewer gratings, subway gratings, mailboxes and even streetlights. A dog that tends to be shy or that is kept at home and on the owner's property almost all the time may exhibit fear of anything he has never seen before. Force the dog to hold his ground, using the SIT, STAY. Praise him warmly. Gradually expose the dog to a wider environment and the specific objects that spook him. Praise him generously for any progress.

Fear of Other Dogs

It's no wonder that some dogs are afraid of other dogs. Some dog owners act as if *our* dirty mongrels will defile *their* precious babies; fear on the part of such people's dogs can be the only result as the owners scoop up their dogs or pull them away in a huff. Play is out of the question.

Dogs who, after leaving the litter, never get to socialize with their own kind can get spooky, fearful and, eventually, aggressive toward any canine they see. While there's no need for your dog to be a social butterfly, all dogs should be able to play with *some* other dogs.

Try to let your dog have at least a pal or two in the neighborhood. Some bitches do not like to be rushed by overzealous males. If this is the case, find a nice lady dog for a play date. Let your dog fool around in the park once in a while. Even a very fearful dog, after a few exposures to gentle dogs of about his own size, can start to become a real dog lover. Do not praise or reward your dog's signs of fear. Try to relax while your dog is making friends, so that he can, too.

Nervousness and Hyperactivity

I don't think you can do too much about severe nervousness or hyperactivity. Usually, it is a breeding or breed problem. Here, definitions *are* important. Lots of people have called me to ask if training would calm down their dogs. Their dogs, it turned out, were very active, normal Terrier puppies. They would like, it turned out, for a five-month-old Fox Terrier to act like a nine-year-old Newfoundland. Training cannot accomplish that.

If you have purchased an active breed or a breed that tends to be high-strung and nervous, or an unusually high-strung, active, noisy, nervous mixed-breed dog, you'll have to learn to love him pretty much the way he is. We cannot turn him into a placid giant, but *some* help is possible.

First, obedience training will help any dog to calm down, act less wild, be more quiet, know his place, know the rules, know some commands and be generally more tractable. If your dog is a nonstop, non-listen machine, obedience training is a must. You will reap very visible rewards for your efforts.

Second, food affects hyperactivity in dogs, just as it does in humans. The hyperactive dog should have more whole grains and less sugar. This eliminates all soft, moist foods from his diet. He should go lighter on meat protein and not eat foods with preservatives, food colorings and sweeteners of any kind. It is more important to be a stickler about his diet than it is with a normally active dog, though good feeding should be a goal with all pets.

Do not feed your hyperactive dog tidbits of birthday cake or pizza, or handfuls of M & M's. A good base food for him would be brown rice. To this, you can add cooked egg, cottage cheese or a small amount of plain, cooked meat and some dry dog chow. Many owners add a multivitamin for dogs and, if his coat is dry, a little vegetable oil.

The third thing to help a hyperactive dog is to give him plenty of outdoor exercise. Often, dogs dubbed as hyperactive are totally normal for their breed, but have been fed a diet high in sugars and food dyes, have not been exercised enough or at all and are totally untrained. Even a placid sporting dog can look hyperactive with that history.

Having a dog is a big responsibility. It takes thought. It takes some time and work. As this book attempts to point out, some of the important things your dog needs will take very little of your time. A better diet takes no more time than a poorer one. Your dog can get exercised by another dog or by your cat, or you can take him along when you run, cycle, walk or skate. You have to oversee his life, though—to make sure he is eating well and exercising, and that he has contact with you and the other members of your family. Then he'll feel loved and secure rather than neglected and hyper. As with the "bad" child who acts out in school, psychological neglect can cause behavior problems in dogs. If your dog gets a bland, whole-grain diet, runs around with the kids for hours, gets petted and brushed near the TV all evening, was well trained and is still a perpetual motion machine, that's probably just the way he's supposed to be—or just the way he *happens* to be—so think of all the fun you'd miss if he'd just lie at the hearth and sleep peacefully.

8

The Noisy Dog

A pest, says the dictionary, is a plant or animal detrimental to man or to his interests.

—Judith Nelson, *Money Saving Garden Magic*

If left alone, he barks until his throat is raw. When someone comes to visit, he barks at them incessantly, until he becomes the center of attention—or gets locked up. If locked up, confined, tied out in the yard, he barks and barks. He whines when he wants something. He yaps when you're sleeping. He talks back when you give a command. He's a noisy dog.

If your dog barks when the bell rings, when someone drives onto your driveway, when the paper boy comes and even when he has to go out or when his water bowl is empty, he is just being a normal dog. It's not his fault if someone comes onto your property at three in the morning. After all, don't you want him to be a noisy dog then? His barking may not suit you one hundred percent of the time, but if it seems to have reasonable cause (protection, to express a need, for fun and the expression of gaiety, for greeting but not for departure), you have no real cause for complaint. However, if his barking, even when reasonably initiated, goes on and on and on, if you cannot quiet him with a word, if he barks at company, if he barks when you fail to pet him or play with him, if he barks in the car or when left alone, then you are dealing with the kind of culprit who can do worse than disturb your sleep and give you a terminal headache. He can infuriate your neighbors, alienate your friends, cause your landlord to institute eviction proceedings and make you wish you had gotten a cat.

Teaching Etiquette Early

Manners should be taught in puppyhood. A small puppy, or even an adult dog, newly adopted, should learn to be quiet when left alone. Small doses of privacy with praise and smiles upon your return gradually make both pup and older dog secure in the fact that you will return and that he has not been abandoned. Some people leave a puppy with both a hot-water bottle (wrapped well in a soft towel to prevent injury) and a ticking clock to replace the warmth of mama and the comforting sound of her heartbeat. If your puppy is comfortable when left alone (he's been fed, he's had water, he's had a chance to relieve himself, he's neither too hot nor too cold), he should not have to cry. If he is given attention before you leave and upon your return, he will learn, as we all do, to accept the inevitable fact that Mommy can't be around every minute of the day.

A dog will associate being left alone with all the things you do just before leaving the house: dressing, putting on makeup, putting on shoes, picking up your car keys, turning on the answering machine, checking the stove, checking the locks, feeding the goldfish, whatever your pattern demands. He knows, too, when he's going and when he isn't because you act differently to him in each case.

Most people chat animatedly with a dog about to be treated to a stroll, asking, "Do you want to go out? Are you ready? Where's your leash?" They tend to ignore the dog who is staying home. Perhaps they feel guilty or are merely distracted or in a rush to get to work.

If you fiddle around with the pattern, it may help your dog adjust. Leaving music playing, something he associates with your presence, can help a dog through his "Oh my God, they left me all alone" anxiety attacks. It's not that the music itself actually soothes him. It's more likely a case of, "If the radio is on, the house retains its master-is-at-home atmosphere."

Another method of teaching the dog to be quiet when left alone is to let him bark it out once or twice. While this usually works rapidly with puppies, it has severe drawbacks with older dogs. First of all, your older dog will not tire quickly like a puppy and he may bark until he injures his throat. Then, there are the neighbors. They may not be willing to put up with the noise while your dog supposedly learns that his barking will not get him the desired result—the return of his master. Their feelings must be considered.

There is a better way to control excessive noise. It's more active, more work, much more exciting. It's the Serendipitous way—interfering with the activity at hand and thereby gaining an automatic right to control it. We are going to teach the noisy dog to make noise on command!

The absolutely insidious thing about poking one little finger into someone else's activity, any activity, is that suddenly you have rights there. When working with dogs, this fact can be very beneficial to both dog and owner.

By taking the most ludicrous course imaginable, your noisy dog will come under your control. Instead of banging on doors, shooting him in the snout with a water gun or letting him bark it out, you are going to note what gets him started and ask him to SPEAK, SPEAK in situations that tend to trigger barking. You'll even reward him for barking when he does it *on command*. This is not like covering for your dog—that is, breaking him when he is about to break on his own. Here we are expanding his vocabulary by naming a natural activity in order to gain control in that area. The reward will come only when he performs that activity, barking, immediately after you issue a command. Soon, your noisy little brat, still noisy indeed, will have begun adding to the noise by barking on command for a dog biscuit or a tidbit of cheese. This is one of the few exceptions where a food reward is appropriate. However, even so, as you keep reinforcing his obedience, begin to vary his reward. At first, the food is a great shortcut. It gets the dog excited, which will make him want to give voice. If you hold the cheese or biscuit out of reach as you say SPEAK, SPEAK, he will be frustrated enough to bark. As he begins to bark readily at your command, praise with warm words, a pat on the head, an occasional food treat. To deeply capture his imagination, the food must be weaned away as soon as possible.

Now you can begin to have some fun with this work. Ask him to SPEAK FOR A BISCUIT, SPEAK TO GO OUT, SPEAK FOR YOUR TOY. Of course, to reinforce, give him what he "asked" for. Now we have a problem dog that does tricks. Is this progress?

Two things have happened. First, your dog began to focus his barking in your direction and do it at your will. Second, since he enjoys barking so much, now he has a legitimate outlet for which he earns praise for his pleasure. You will now institute a third change. Now you will not only start him barking, but you will stop him as well. Remember, the focus is now on you.

Now, as part of his trick, ask him to SPEAK FOR THE BIS-CUIT, praise him when he does, tell him ENOUGH in a firm voice and drop the biscuit into his mouth. This gives him instant success and no choice but to obey the turn-off command. Practice this step for about one week. So far, you have put in two or three weeks and you still have a noisy dog. Continue to work with him, finding new and clever ways to implement ENOUGH, because this, as you can see, is pay dirt. If he speaks to go out, he must be quiet as soon as you get him out. You can make a leash correction and tell him ENOUGH if he continues to bark. If he speaks for a dog biscuit, the biscuit quiets him. If he barks for water, he'll be still while drinking. If he keeps barking while drinking, drop everything and call Johnny Carson.

You can now begin to use ENOUGH when your dog barks and you have not been the motivation for his speech. If he barks at the front door, first tell him GOOD BOY. He should bark when some-one approaches your door. If he continues to bark once you are there to open the door, tell him ENOUGH. What he has to learn now is that you want a warning of two or three woofs and then silence. So, don't forget to praise the barking and then follow with ENOUGH. Now we are back where we started. We have a noisy dog barking his head off at the front door. The difference is that now you have a language and the ability to make him focus on you. If he does not heed your command, ENOUGH, now you can zap him. Grasp his collar. Shake him once or twice from side to side, repeating BAD DOG, ENOUGH. Immediately place him on a SIT, STAY. Repeat the correction if he repeats his noisemaking. This should begin to work soon because of the foundation you patiently laid with trick work.

Your yappy little Yorkie will never become a quiet Newf. In fact, even though the barking gets to you sometimes, you bought him for what he is—an active, bouncy, yippy little dog. Even if you have to say ENOUGH to quiet him each time you go to the door, and it works, you're doing very well. Don't expect him to know, each time, all by himself, that after two barks he should button his lip. That would be too much to ask. Of course, there are times when button his lip is *all* you want. In those cases, you will work to teach him to ENOUGH *before* he begins to bark.

If you confine your dog (let's say you're painting), he should accept it quietly—grudgingly, but quietly. If he barks then, *do not praise him*. Tell him ENOUGH, sternly and seriously. If he continues to bark, go to him, grasp his collar and shake him, repeating ENOUGH. Even if you lose your patience, do not let him out while he is barking. That will only reinforce exactly what you want to be rid of—his attitude that if he barks, the world is his.

The element of surprise can work wonders with barking dogs. When caught by surprise, they will always shut up, at least for a moment. While a shake using his collar or the collar and leash is the best, most humane correction, excessive barking can be tenacious and you should have more than one trick up your sleeve. You can use noise to surprise him. Sometimes banging on the door will work. You can use water. It's messy but effective. Use a pail of it if he's outside and no longer a puppy. Catch him right in the chops with the water in the middle of a bark. Then praise him immediately for quieting down. Sputtering doesn't count as noise.

Indoors, you can use a water gun if the collar shake doesn't get to your noisy dog. There are dogs, of course, for whom eight or ten different methods won't work. Yours may be one of those. If so, you'll have to be creative. This is great as long as your correction is not mean or unfair. One thing to watch out for, as you work, is that some dogs, like some kids, will do anything for attention. They may even prefer negative attention to none at all. For those dogs, a non-face-to-face correction such as banging on the door is preferable to the shake, which may make the dog feel he won because he made you come back. Whatever you try, watch the dog's reactions carefully and you will know if the correction is working or not, if it is too hard or too soft. What's right for someone else's dog may be all wrong for yours. In this, as in all dog work, you must monitor the dog. He is where all the answers can be found.

Barking When Left Alone

With all your patient work, your dog may *still* bark when you leave the house. He may have good reasons to do so: he may hear the postman, the meter reader, the newsboy, another dog barking,

the buzzer next door, the elevator stopping on your floor, the door
to the compactor room opening, the phone ringing, cars passing, a
bird singing, clouds rolling by, dust settling. He may be high-strung,
a little overzealous in protecting home and hearth while you are out,
easily ticked off or just a spoiled brat who barks because he's not getting his way. Who cares? The neighbors who call the police or your
landlord don't care. Moving isn't the answer unless you can afford
an island. He's got to be stopped.

Your foundation work will help a lot in your new task. At least
you have the language and have taught the dog to focus. This is all-
important. Now you must make your dog feel that you are going
away—ignore him, dress to go out, turn on the answering machine,
kiss the hamster, goldfish and Abyssinian good-bye, pat him on his
worried head and go. You may even have to drive away—a piece—
and walk back. You have to be convincing—and patient. Some dogs
bark the minute you leave. Some mutter under their breaths for an
hour or so and then begin the heavy-duty noisemaking. If yours is
the latter, take a good book and some sandwiches and camp out
where you can hear him but he can't smell you.

We have been told not to correct a dog unless he is caught in the
act or there is evidence of his crime—but how can we get in and correct the noisy dog without startling him into silence? We can't. Instead, to keep his focus on his crime, as soon as you hear him barking, yell NO, NO, NO and keep it up until you have unlocked your
door, grabbed your surprised dog and given him a really good shaking by the collar. Now, without so much as a "So long, toots," you
will depart again and resume your post, reading and sandwich eating. And you will wait.

If the dog resumes his noisemaking, you will again shout NO,
NO, NO and rush in upon him, this time shaking him even harder
and longer so that he begins to *wish* you'd go to work and leave him
alone. Without praise, conversation or guilt, exit center stage and resume your chore. You can easily see that (1) this will work and (2)
this will take a commitment of your time. Weekdays, unless you are
on vacation, will not do.

Most dogs I have worked with have learned rather quickly that
sounding off when left alone will lead to no good. Bravo for our
team. When this procedure was followed and stuck to without
guilty relaxing of the rule of silence, the correction worked. If you
do it one day and give in to the dog the next, as many people do,

the dog will keep barking and whining, waiting and hoping for those days when it will get him the company and attention he wants. He will grow more spoiled and more noisy, not less. Consistency, as always, is essential for success.

An additional trick you can use to correct excessive noise is to make a short line or tiny leash that can hang on your dog's collar like a handle. It can be very helpful for any number of corrections because, when used, it feels like a normal leash correction to the dog. When you are at home, let it dangle from his collar and use it when you have to make a correction. If your dog barks when left alone in the house, leave a flat leather collar and the tiny leash on him when you depart. All you need is a leash clip with about two or three inches of cord hanging from it so that you have something to grab. The weight of the tiny leash is enough to remind the dog that you can make a good correction if he is a bad dog. If indeed you have to rush in and correct him, you can grasp the short line to implement the collar shake. Then, when you leave again, the small dangling leash is a constant reminder of your power. Be sure before leaving the leash on your dog that you have used it first and that he is not attempting to chew it. Foreign matter can't do his innards any good.

While working on noise pollution, canine style, please do inform your neighbors (if they have complained) that you are correcting the matter and will need a little patience from them while your dog learns. If you have a dog-loving, easygoing neighbor, do ask for some feedback so you'll know if all your hard work is successfully quieting the dog. An honest, friendly neighbor can be very helpful when you are correcting this kind of problem. If the barking has already caused legal proceedings and you are adamant about correcting it and not packing up and moving West, then, in the absence of a helpful neighbor, try leaving a tape recorder with a long tape on. As you work, with a lot of sweat and a little luck, you'll be coming home soon to listen to two hours of silence with an occasional passing car or phone ringing.

Caveats

Some people are enamored of shortcuts, no matter what the cost. To cater to their wants, shock collars that are triggered by sound to give the dog a moderate shock when he barks are available. I do not believe in using such gimmicks, for several reasons. The first and most important reason for using time, training and patience is that what you really want is an educated dog who will focus on you and obey you. Second, many dogs are badly bred and may be nervous or high-strung, particularly those with a noisemaking problem. The collar can only make a nervous dog more so. The third reason is that in most cases when amateurs (and some professionals) fool around with gadgets that are supposed to give an electric shock to a dog, they do not know how to regulate the shock and may harm the dog, do nothing to the dog or get shocked themselves. Shortcuts often have hidden disadvantages. Don't be tempted.

Spoiled Barking

Spoiled barking is another story. Merely working on quieting your dog is not enough. If he's spoiled, it will just come out in another place. You can *smell* when a dog is spoiled. No one really has to tell you. He just behaves as if his rights are more important than your rights. In fact, he's not too clear that you have rights at all. Most people spoil tiny dogs. It's not hard to see why. We tend to buy tiny dogs because they are so cute, cuddly and carryable. We want a little baby doll to primp and spoil. That was the appeal in the first place. Then, when we find we do not like the results of our work, a tyrannical brat in a rhinestone collar, what can we do? Should you yell at a half pint? Should you hit a three-pound dog? Certainly not. Should you train the little peanut? Of course.

If your dog barks and barks when he wants attention, barks and carries on when company comes until they pet him, sleeps in your bed, talks back when you give a command, walks on your furniture, eats special foods and weighs ten pounds or less, he's spoiled. The barking he's doing is just symptomatic of a greater ill. By the way, your spoiled little dog may weigh one hundred and fifty pounds. So don't go away.

A spoiled dog must be trained. Once trained, a dog can be spoiled with no harm done. Training is the language by which you establish yourself as leader. Once elected, you can be the kindest leader on earth and your spoiled dog will never be a spoiled brat. Step one is basic obedience training. Step two, which can be done simultaneously, is the Serendipitous Method of teaching your dog to bark on command and silence himself on command. Step three, if necessary, is a little bit of correction for barking when he shouldn't even start; when he's left alone, given a command, not getting attention. This gives you a nice, spoiled dog. Not a bad pet.

Barking in the Car

Some dogs get noisy when they are in a moving vehicle. They may be afraid. They may get extremely overprotective, barking when someone nears the car or at every passing *enemy* when the car is moving. Some distinguish between cabs, passenger vehicles and panel trucks. Some find only motorcycles detestable. Any way you slice it, having them in the back seat makes for a rough trip. Some dogs whine or sing when in the car because they get very excited. Often, these dogs are high-strung or very sensitive. A ride is associated with something thrilling—a trip to a dog show, a long outing, an adventure of some kind. They just cannot contain themselves. They make noise to prove it.

I find that noisemaking in the car is the hardest to stop. First of all, the car and the things passing it are a constant stimulation to the dog. His focus is not on you. Secondly, you are physically in an awkward position to make any kind of correction. Many dogs will stop whatever annoying noise they are making as soon as you stop the car. So if you stop to make a correction, they stop and you have nothing to correct. If you have someone else drive, it might help, but some dogs wise up to the fact that you can then make corrections, so they choose those rides to be quiet.

The safest way to travel with a dog is to crate him. If a crate will fit in the back of your car, you might get some good results by tossing a towel over the crate so that the dog does not see the passing cars and trucks. By all means, teach the dog to bark on command and to stop barking when you say ENOUGH. If the stimulation which makes him bark is moderate, the command may quiet him until his barking response is provoked again, or it may quiet him for five or ten minutes each time you say it. Eventually, he will quiet down for longer and longer stretches.

Sometimes the excitement of the car or the passing scenery will make the dog freaky and he will seem not to hear commands nor to be able to focus. In this case, someone should sit in the back seat with the dog and grasp his collar when he begins to bark or whine. The command ENOUGH should be given. If he doesn't stop, repeat the command and give the dog a shake or two by the collar. If he's quiet for even a moment, praise and reassure him. Expect progress to be slow. Look hard for *legitimate* opportunities to praise the dog and to feel pleased with your own work.

Vary the time you work according to what the dog's problem is and how it manifests itself. Some dogs will whine or bark initially and then quiet down after a five- or ten-minute drive. With these dogs, you should always work long enough so that you can express your pleasure to the dog when he rides quietly. Other dogs begin quietly and, the longer the ride, the more frenzied they become. When this is the case, do your training rides when you have stops to make close to home. Work a few minutes into the frenzy so that you can calm the dog and praise him for quieting down. In either case, integrate your training rides with trips you'd make normally in order to save time, money, gasoline and wear and tear on your vehicle.

The Protection Bonus

As long as you've done the work of teaching your dog to bark on command, you might as well get an extra benefit for your effort. There are times when it is very handy to have a dog who will bark on command. Most often, when there is a threat of danger, a barking dog is enough clout to scare away a potential thief. In fact, if the dog is barking behind closed doors, he doesn't even have to be of formidable size to do the trick. Why should a thief bother tangling with a dog of any size and risking a bite when he could work elsewhere in peace and quiet.

The only drawback to the work you have done so far when you need it for protection is that no thief in his right mind would be afraid of a dog that barked when you told him SPEAK, SPEAK. All you have to do to eliminate that giveaway is to switch the dog to a hand signal. This can be easily and quickly done with any command, as you already know if you have obedience-trained your dog. Each time you tell the dog to speak, point your finger at him. After a few days, point the finger and do not use the verbal command. If he has not absorbed the hand signal yet, it will be clear to you. He won't bark. Tell him NO, SPEAK and make sure he is focused on your finger. Now, once he will bark when you point at him, you can say anything you please to start him barking. For example, you can point your finger at him and say WHO'S THERE? WATCH HIM! WATCH HIM! If a thief hears that and then hears a dog bark, he will assume that you have a protection dog and he will depart. Of course, the thief will not depart if he has singled you out because you have something valuable he wants. So if you happen to own the Hope Diamond or a pair of Gucci shoes you may want a burglar alarm and Pinkerton guards as well as a barking dog.

This same protection trick can be used when you are walking your dog or are caught in the elevator with an unsavory person. But in this case, the size of the dog will count. In a frightening situation such as this, a tank and guns would be preferable, but it is unlikely that the thief will notice your hand signal and, if you are stuck and need help, the barking dog gimmick certainly beats nothing.

9

Destructiveness

One sprinkles the most sugar where the tart is burnt.

—Dutch proverb

It is perfectly natural for a dog to use his powerful jaws for chewing, tearing, shredding, gnawing and chomping. He'll do this, just like us only more so, for fun as well as for sustenance. It's just as natural for him to dig. He's built to do it pretty well without the help of a shovel and he's got energy to burn. Digging outside will get him a cooler spot in which to lie down on a hot day. If, after he does it, your azalea falls down dead, roots exposed to the blazing sun, that wasn't part of his plan. He was just trying to get comfortable.

Perhaps you have the outstanding luck to have a dog who digs in the middle of your couch. One swell Doberman I knew did it one day after being teased by the family's Siamese cat. The cat took refuge under the low-slung couch, knowing that the dog she frustrated couldn't squeeze under it. Unable to use the obvious, logical route, he created a logical route of his own—straight down from the top.

Some dogs do double whammies to the furniture. First, you give the dog a nice, greasy knucklebone. When you get busy again, he takes his prize and proceeds to feast on the couch. Some time later, he's resting his weary body on the couch again and *voilà!* he smells bone. If a dog smells bone and there's no bone in sight, he knows it must be buried, right? So he digs for it.

If your dog eats couches, plants, underwear, windowsills, parts of your kid's bicycle (I kid you not), you'll want to correct these inappropriate habits. Destructiveness can be tricky to correct and can recur sometimes, after a long hiatus of good behavior. It will take more effort to correct this problem than many other dog problems, but if you just shake your head and mutter "Dogs will be dogs," eventually you'll tire of gritting your teeth all the way to the poorhouse and you may feel like strangling your dog instead of correcting him. There are a few milder and more realistic approaches which will protect both house and dog—house from dog and dog from you!

Prevention When Possible—It's Cheaper!

I don't know anyone who ever raised a puppy without losing a shoe, a glove, a table leg, the padding from under the oriental, a pet cat, *something*. Unless you raise your dogs in a kennel, they are exposed to the house and it to them when they are puppies. This means that the infamous chewing stage will cost you. Consider this a program to educate the puppy and *cut down* on losses. I'd like to promise to cut them out entirely, but no one's perfect.

First, rush out and buy a crate. It is costly, but less so than a couch. If you didn't buy one for housebreaking, reconsider now. I would not consider raising a puppy without one.

The crate will be more than a helpful tool in your dog's education. It will ensure the continuation of his life with your family. When things are bad, when you're doing everything right and he's doing everything wrong, you'll have a place to stash him when you have to leave him alone. That way, you can return home to no surprises. Your couch will be intact. Your walls and wallpaper will remain ungashed. Your shoes will be wearable. You'll be able to wholeheartedly love your puppy and continue training him. An untrained, untrustworthy puppy just should not have the run of the house or access to anything he can damage unless you are watching him and can use his *attempt* as an excuse to educate.

A sound prevention program would include crating the puppy when no one is monitoring him, obedience work daily (particularly right before leaving the puppy alone), fair, clear corrections and a good supply of chew toys.

Did You Do That?

When you are home and the puppy is wandering around whatever room you are in, he should be corrected easily and matter-of-factly for chewing on the molding, for example. Grasp his collar firmly and pull him back, hit the *molding* with your hand to make a noise and focus his attention on it and scold him by saying NO, NO, NO, DID YOU DO THAT? Immediately give him a chew toy, one that's lying around for him to have whenever he likes, saying OK, GOOD BOY. By replacing a NO, NO with a YES, YES, the dog can still satisfy his urge to chew (Serendipity again) and, at the same time, is getting a small dose of education. It will take many doses for him to get the hang of what he can and can't chew. So, for a few months, you should watch him and use every transgression calmly as an opportunity to teach. That is easier to do if the dog is prevented from major war crimes such as eating the couch than if he is free to maraud and plunder while you are out working hard in order to bring home the dog food.

Train Daily, Train Hard

Another essential ingredient for proper destructiveness control is obedience work. From this, you two will have a common language and your dog will learn how to listen, look attentively into your eyes when you speak and, above all, take you seriously. If he doesn't take you seriously, how can you hope to convince him to keep his teeth off your tasty furniture. In addition to all the other benefits of obedience work, you will also use it just before leaving the dog alone. In this way, he's gotten outside, he's had your alpha dog position reinforced right before you left the house, he's relieved himself before the lesson, he's had some exercise during and after the lesson and he's had some attention before being left all alone. The fairness gets through. This works.

On the days you fly out, late, harried, too busy to do anything with the dog, you may come home to find an unwanted present: confetti in the color your couch used to be (unless you have a crate). Spite? I think not. It's that old, rotten feeling—anxiety. A little contact, a little work, a small correction here and there and something of his own to chew work better than Valium. Eventually, he will have your message down pat and will be able to gnaw on a toy and behave admirably out of the crate when you are out of the house, but be cautious and don't rush toward this step.

Let the Correction Fit the Crime

Suppose your dog is not a puppy, has been trained, gets a nice romp before you go to work and still tries to eat his way through walls or floors. You'll have to ask yourself: Does my dog have too much freedom for his personal level of responsibility? (Yes) and Are my corrections clear and firm enough? (Probably not).

First, then, you will want to follow the routine of training before leaving and then go back to confining the dog where he can do no damage. With dog or puppy, freedom should be offered in small doses at first, with careful monitoring of the dog's behavior and scrupulous correcting of all transgressions. Then, freedom can be increased if the dog is not doing any damage during the time he is out and running around the house. He should always be praised for good behavior. At any sign of a backslide (and all dogs do have them), go back to full confinement after correcting the dog at the scene of his crime so that he knows why he is being confined.

Firmer correction means taking the dog to the object he destroyed, banging *it* or shaking *it* in his face (depending on what it is), shaking him by the collar, verbally chewing him out and then confining him. For a chronic adult chewer, use the same object for five days in a row instead of waiting for new destruction. You have the evidence—do not discard it—and his scent is on it. Rediscover it each day for five days and correct him and confine him as you did the first day. Confinement should last at least one hour and no one should baby talk to him or feed him treats in sympathy during this time.

While I do approve of scolding a dog who has destroyed household goods or clothing, and I do feel that confinement as a correction works and is a clear and humane way to train a dog, I do not at all believe in treating the untrained dog as an outcast or being cruel or sadistic to him. I have heard dog owners (some of whom would not use a crate for fear it was too cruel) talk of not feeding a dog as a punishment. Sending a dog to bed without his supper is no way to train a dog, nor is it fair or humane. The dog cannot care for his own needs without your help. While you might not feel like going out and giving the dog a refresher course in HEEL, SIT, DOWN, COME and STAY the day after he ate your couch, that's *precisely* what he needs. Do not forgo training because your dog made a mistake. When calm and recovered, go train your dog, with patience, kindness and a firm hand.

Continue the pattern of training, confinement and corrections when needed. Move slowly toward freedom and feel secure that one day your dog will be reliable enough to be left alone safely without being confined. Try to keep your expectations reasonable so that you will not give him freedom when he cannot handle it well. If you take him on vacation with you or visiting, if you move to a new residence or have a major change in schedule or lifestyle, develop the ability to have a dog's-eye view of things. In this way, you will be able to predict and avoid canine anxiety attacks, backslides and losses due to destructive chewing.

If you find that the chewing problem persists and you are doing all of the above, your dog may be sadly lacking in exercise and just burning off energy any way he can. If he's got ants in his pants and you hardly ever run him or let him play hard with other dogs, he may just need longer outings and more leg stretching before the destructiveness problem is finally solved. With all the possibilities available, surely one that suits him will fit your timetable and lifestyle. It is because of the fact that a destructiveness problem is affected by so many factors that it can be tricky to solve.

Dealing With Specifics

PLANT EATING: There are two ways to correct plant eating. One way is to correct the dog every time he does it. The other is to try that a few times and if the dog seems addicted, overly persistent or uniquely slow to learn, hang the plants in a beautiful pattern in front of your windows and stop worrying. Unless your dog is doing lots of things you don't like, or his plant eating is part of a whole package of spoiled behavior that needs correction anyway, I'd take the expedient way out.

If you think that's weak and cowardly, here are twenty-one reasons why that's not so—a list of common household plants poisonous to dogs:

COMMON PLANTS POISONOUS TO DOGS

1. Autumn Crocus
2. Azaleas
3. Bleeding Heart
4. Buttercups
5. Castor Bean
6. Daffodil
7. Dutchman's Breeches
8. Elderberry
9. Foxglove
10. Golden Chain
11. Hyacinth
12. Iris
13. Jack-in-the-pulpit
14. Larkspur
15. Lily of the Valley
16. Mistletoe
17. Narcissus
18. Oleander
19. Poinsettia
20. Rhubarb
21. Yew

If your dog ingests any of these plants, indoors, or out, call your veterinarian immediately.

HOLE DIGGING: "A hole is nothing, but you can break your neck in it."—Austin O'Malley, *Keystones of Thought*

I have read some gruesome corrections for hole digging. I surely wouldn't do any of them to my dog or yours. Neither, I bet, would you. I prefer a sane and softer approach. First, sorry, the dog must be trained. If so, he'll hear you when you bellow. Believe it or not (you may know it already), you can carry on like a lunatic and not change the dog's behavior one bit when he's not obedience trained. That's because he doesn't *hear* you. He simply has not learned how to listen.

Dog digs. Tell him NO. Dog digs. Grasp the collar, pull him back from the hole, saying NO. Dog digs. Grasp collar and shake him, telling him NO, NO as you do. Repeat when necessary. Fill in holes in between or silently thank the dog for doing your work and plant trees in them. Remember, as you train, that dogs sometimes dig to find a cool spot to lie in. If your dog is out on a hot day, make sure he has some shade and a bucket full of cool water. You might just prevent a hole or two.

There's another way. Dogs love to dig. If it weren't for our reasonable desire to have a pretty garden, it wouldn't matter. You can divide your yard. Keep most of it for yourself—the sun, the shade, the front, the front of the back—whatever you like. Give a piece to the dog. Pen it, fence it or put in an overhead run. You keep your yard the way you like it. He'll keep his the way he likes it. Every other day you'll hand your kids a quarter and the poop scoop and they'll keep his area sanitary. Not a bad compromise?

SCRATCHING DOORS: This is a pip of a problem. You confine your dog to get your point across and he scratches the wallpaper, the doors, the moldings. Of course, a crate would prevent this, but eventually he must be out of the crate and he may still persist in his penchant for paint removal if ever you close a door against his will.

There are several corrections you can try to stop this costly habit. All you are trying to do, in this and any correction, is to find the thing that turns your dog around, the thing that makes an activity that was fun for him no longer worth doing. Negative attention might work for your dog. When you leave or confine him and he begins to whine or bark and scratch the door, you can bang on the door and yell NO. If he persists, usually after a short break, you can open the door, bang on the area he scratched, grasp his collar and shake him and enunciate the immortal words DID YOU DO THAT? Yet, even repeated for several weeks when necessary, this might not work for *your* dog.

You can try balloons. Buy a package of party balloons, blow up a dozen or so, tie them off and tape them to the inside of the door your dog scratches. The balloons themselves might spook him. If not, once he tries scratching the door, at least one balloon is sure to pop. The noise and wind can work as a nifty correction when you are not even home. You can even pop a balloon before you leave. In that case, he might not even give the door one tentative try. Dogs do not like sudden, loud noises.

RERUN CHEWING: This does not mean the dog ate the Sony. It refers to ritualistic chomping on the same old thing or the same old spot. Some dogs just seem to have a thing for one corner of your rug or one leg of one table. Often, their obsession centers on your five-thousand-dollar Steinway or your handmade Chinese area rug. If it were something cheap, you might not even notice it.

Certain acts can become habitual, like lighting a cigarette when the phone rings. In order to break your dog's habit, a pattern must be broken, a link taken out of a chain of events. With dogs, the best cure for rerun chewing is to separate the dog from the object for several weeks. I do not suggest putting your piano into storage. Instead, confine the dog to another area for a limited time.

There are also products which are meant to discourage chewing. Unfortunately, though, for every dog discouraged by a bitter taste, there's at least one who couldn't care less. Experiment. Improvise. Invent. Even fifty repetitions of a correction might leave your dog unmoved. The most important thing this book can teach you is the reasoning behind corrections, not just the mechanical process. Like my friend, Adele, who covered her couch with aluminum foil, someplace along the line you may have to work out your own teaching methods, just to suit your dog. Don't be afraid to try, nor to give up a correction that is not working and press on to a new one. As long as you are humane, whatever works is good dog training.

10

Transitions: Helping Your Dog Muddle Through Major Changes in Your Life and His

Any change, even a change for the better, is always accompanied by drawbacks and discomforts.

—Arnold Bennett, *The Arnold Bennett Calendar*

When you are spackling up nail holes and tripping over cartons or mopping up after the new puppy or figuring out which end of your new baby the diaper goes on, you may already be on overload. Who has time to worry about good old Fido? He does. Therefore, you must, too.

Transitions are difficult enough for humans who can, at least, use their powers of reasoning to figure out, more or less, how to muddle through. Your dog, poor baby, doesn't know why you are moving from two blocks away from his favorite swimming hole to the big city or why you brought a new dog into the house for him to be jealous of or why all your attention is going to the new baby and not to him.

You can't sit down with your dog and have a heart-to-heart. If you try, he'll love the contact but it won't make the transition any smoother for him. However, there are ways to handle major changes that will make things easier and more palatable for both you and your dog.

Moving to a New Den

To a dog, familiarity breeds contentment. When moving to a new residence, it is wise to pack an emergency box for your dog, a box that will be unpacked early on, if not first. The sight of his bowls in a new kitchen, his bed in a new bedroom, his toys on a strange floor, will help him to begin to understand that this unfamiliar place which doesn't smell like home is home indeed. You can also communicate reassuringly to him via the familiarity of *your* things. Even before the movers arrive, if you can slip your old den area rug into your new den, he'll begin to get the message.

If your move is not over a great distance, it can help if your dog gets to go along once or twice when you go to measure for carpeting and wait (and wait) for the telephone company. Praise him for entering, sniffing around (of course, let him explore and get familiar) and eating dinner in his new home. If he needs to trail around after you, let him—and praise him for that, too. When I moved back to the city from the suburbs, my dog, Oliver, came along one day to watch me wash dishes and hang pictures. The interruptions for fun and games helped us both. We shared a picnic lunch on the floor of the empty apartment. We played hide and seek to get familiar with the lay of the land. I taught him to go to each room by name, a game which gave him much pleasure in his old home. It was only afterward that he was relaxed enough to dig into his supply of rawhide bones, already stashed in the hall closet.

A move from the city to the suburbs may mean teaching a dog to relieve himself on grass rather than pavement. More difficult is the move from country to city. In this case, and sometimes in the other, you'll have to treat the transition as a housebreaking problem. Put your dog on a fairly rigid walking schedule, walking him on time in the new, designated area, and praise him if he catches on. If he doesn't, return him home and wait for the next walk. Do not take him out every hour "just so he gets the idea." If necessary, confine him to one small area between walks so that he is forced to make the change you want—outdoors.

Taking the time to walk around your new neighborhood with your dog will help him get his sea legs and make the change fun for him. Since you have to do it anyway, when you go out hunting for a new dry cleaner, drugstore, bank and hardware store, take your dog along on the search. Once acquainted with the new area, he'll behave better outdoors, look forward to his outings and pull enthusiastically when you near what is now his new home. When transitions are tough on you, his company will give you that sense of comfort and familiarity that relaxes *you* and makes changing homes a little easier on the soul.

Try to arrange your time so that you will not have to leave your dog alone in his new quarters the first day. When you begin to leave him there, praise him when you say good-bye, make the first few outings brief and pet him lavishly when you return. Replacing a lost, pleasant ritual with a new one can do wonders. If he can look forward to a dip at a new swimming hole or an elaborate evening stroll to a nearby park, he'll soon feel comfortable and secure in his new setting. Time, praise and a little ingenuity can get the job done.

Sibling Rivalry, Canine Style

If your dog is an "only child," you might think he'd welcome a new dog into the fold—a friend, a playmate, a confidant. In a way, he would—that is, until he figures out that he has to share *you* with the other dog. If you plan to add a second dog to please your dog, think twice. He might be better off with play dates with the dog down the block rather than losing the spotlight to a charming and demanding new puppy. Anyway, you'll be the one stuck with all the extra work, housebreaking chores and training.

If, on the other hand, you want a second dog for *you*, your first dog will have an adjustment to make, not unlike the adjustment a first child has to make when he loses his treasured only-child status to a sibling. Common sense will help a lot. The first dog should still get attention first, meals first, greeted first, fussed over first. Once he feels he hasn't lost his special place in your family, attention can be paid to the puppy without wounding your older dog's feelings.

Diplomacy may necessitate a little fiddling around. How come the puppy gets three meals a day and he only gets one? You can withhold a few handfuls of his food at his chow time and feed him a snack when the puppy chows down. Don't feed him *extra* food, or he'll replace jealousy with obesity.

Be sure to separate the dogs periodically. A young puppy can be very pesty to an older dog. Even if the dogs get on well and enjoy playing, the puppy will become very dependent on the older dog if he doesn't get to stay home alone and also go out alone. Your first dog also needs time alone, individual outings, quiet times with just your company and other pleasant remembrances of things past. Try not to change every aspect of his lifestyle even though there's a new dog in the house.

And Baby Makes Four

Many people fret unnecessarily about the addition of a baby to their dog's life. In their anxiety, they may punish the dog or yell at him for normal curiosity. Alternately, they may allow the dog to become overprotective when the baby is around, enjoying the fact that he won't let anyone near the new infant. Both tactics can foreshadow a one-way trip to the pound.

Expect a lot from your dog and help him to come through with flying colors. Unless you have strong reason to expect aggressive behavior (and if you do, that should be taken care of, baby or no baby), you should assume that, given an extra dose of love and affection, your dog will happily accept your little lamb into his flock. Animals usually love the young of any species and most dogs are naturally gentle with "new" creatures. Let your dog sniff the baby and praise him for doing so. Including him in this joy will help him to continue to feel good and lessen his desire to steal attention by being naughty, just like a jealous sibling.

Some dogs pester when baby is getting nursed, a difficult time for you to make corrections. Save a special toy for these occasions, a favorite bone or fresh rawhide chip for him to nurse on. Also, teach him GO LIE DOWN. DOWN means "drop" right where you are. GO LIE DOWN means do it anywhere but here, a bonus for busy people and baby feeders alike. It is taught after the dog knows the DOWN command by (1) leashing him; (2) pointing to an area across the room; (3) commanding GO LIE DOWN enthusiastically; and (4) running him to the spot as you repeat the command. Once he's there and down, praise him like mad. After learning this new command, the dog is unlikely to resent the separation from you that it causes. On the contrary, getting and executing a command will make him feel accomplished and pleased.

Kids and Dogs: Safety First

Dogs and kids are a natural combination. As your baby grows, both dog and baby will have to learn how to behave appropriately around each other. In some circumstances, you must protect your child from your dog. In others, you must protect your dog from your child. After some patience and a little work, the lives of both can be enriched by the bond they share with each other.

Sometimes the natural behavior of a dog is at odds with the way you want your child treated. To a dog's mind, if it's on the floor, it's his. If *it* happens to be the pickle that slithered off your plate to the kitchen floor, *it* will more than likely be resting comfortably in your dog's stomach before you can retrieve it. If *it* is your crawling baby, your dog, untrained, may treat baby like another dog. This can mean mouthing, nipping and tugging on clothes. A few well placed NO's should teach any nice dog his limits.

When baby gets older and a little tougher, he's apt to be a menace to your dog. At two, he'll pull fur, tug at ears, poke little fingers in eyes, slam his toy truck onto your sleeping pet. Young children need supervision when playing with dogs. A small child can't be expected to control the behavior of a dog, large or small. Nor can he always control his own impulses or understand that the big, hairy "toy" has feelings, too.

When children get a little older, they tend to smother dogs with affection. This is particularly true when there are several children in the family. Unless you have a dog for each, when one child plays with Fido, he'll become the main attraction. A dog getting piled on by three kids at a time is apt to panic. He may, despite his good breeding, try to defend himself. Some simple ground rules help. A dog should never be cornered, followed into his under-the-table retreat or trapped on the bottom of a heap of giggling siblings.

Puppies love to steal children's toys. In this case, you'll have to step in and monitor the puppy's behavior. Like kids, puppies will focus on objects that feel good, taste good, smell good and get lots of attention, like that favorite teddy bear. When the kids run after a puppy, he thinks it's a game. Teddy in mouth, he'll dash around the dining room table. The more the kids yell and run, the more fun the puppy will have, the more rewarded he'll feel for stealing. If your puppy is obedient, don't chase him, but call him. Grasp the toy, telling him OUT, take it and praise him, even if he puts up a small fight. He'll catch on. If he's not obedient (too young, not yet trained, just plain full of the devil), tie a long string to his collar at play time, making sure you are around to see that it doesn't get tangled and hurt him. Now when he gets a mouth full of toys and takes off to tease the kids, call him to come. If he's on the far side of the table, ready to dash away and keep his treasures as long as possible, pick up the end of the string and give a tug. He'll catch on.

It's awfully hard on dogs to watch children tearing back and forth, as children are apt to do, and not get in on the fun. Some will let their herding instincts take over. They'll nip feet and pull at clothing as the kids go whizzing by. When your puppy gets wild, teach the kids to freeze. This alone may stop the herding and nipping. Let them run again, with you watching. This time, if puppy herds and nips, reprimand him with a sharp NO and a shake by his collar. If he still continues, separate him from the kids for a while by crating him or confining him to another room. In this way, you'll be teaching him his limits and some important manners, and the kids will learn how to minimize his mini attacks as best they can.

Just as Fido must learn to respect the rights of your children and their property, so must they learn to respect his rights and his things. First, they should let sleeping dogs lie. For some dogs, being startled into a wakeful state may get more than their dander up. It may raise hackles, too. If the kids want to play and the dog is having a catnap, they are better off calling him than pouncing on him. This kind of respect can't hurt your own lazy Sunday mornings either.

While it's best not to fuss with a dog who's in the middle of dinner, you should have your dog trained to accept this kind of interference, just for emergencies. When he's little, tell him OK whenever he gets his food. Then, with his leash on, tell him NO one day when you put down his bowl. If he waits, give him a fast OK and praise him. If he lunges for his chow, jerk him back with his leash and repeat NO. If he now waits, tell him OK and praise him. Once this routine is established and he will wait for his release word, try taking the food away in the middle of a meal. If he growls or complains, scold him and don't give him back his dinner. If he's reasonable about the whole procedure, give the dish right back, telling him OK, GOOD BOY. This kind of training shouldn't be practiced more than once or twice a week so as not to make the dog frantic about losing his food. Once he's trustworthy, you won't have to worry about the kids handling him while he's eating.

While you're thinking safety for kids and dogs, the kids should learn when and when not to handle other people's dogs. Since they love their own, they might think it's fine to rush up to and handle any dog they see. Some dogs abhor being handled by children.

Basically, no dog that is alone should be handled—a tethered dog, a stray, a fenced dog, a dog waiting politely outside a store or in a car. Sometimes the situation itself will trigger the dog's protective instincts. Besides, there's no one around to tell you that he's friendly and good with kids. If the owner is around, children should ask if they may pet the dog. Safety ensured, a nice friendship may ensue.

If a dog is hurt, even your own, it's better to let an adult do the handling. Unless the kids are older and experienced, they may unwittingly hurt the dog. An injured dog, beside himself in pain, may bite just because he's hurting and confused. Once bitten, the kids may harbor a long-term fear of dogs, a sad situation which can usually be avoided.

Fear of dogs which stems from an unfortunate experience with an aggressive dog can often be allayed with sensitive handling and gentle encouragement, but sometimes a child's fears have little to do with a real experience. Sometimes the unconscious plays tricks. The dog may become a symbol for the rage and aggression that the child himself feels and for which he has no outlet. Since his feelings are taboo, he'll feel guilty about them and may try to place them elsewhere. He may fancy that angry dogs wish to bite him because he's bad. Naturally, this kind of fear is harder to assuage than the other. But some understanding talk about feelings and some low-key contact with gentle dogs can often turn the tables. Even if a child chooses not to share bed and teddy bear with a canine, it's nice to feel on friendly terms with creatures so abundantly present in our society.

Another unusual phenomenon can occur when a new dog joins the family. Everyone will fuss over the puppy. He'll be fed often, watched, admired and carried around. He'll be the center of attention. To the youngest child, a puppy may be every bit as much a threat as a new baby in the house. If your child feels that he's lost the spotlight, that he's no longer the baby, he may get very jealous. Signs of this strange kind of sibling rivalry can be both obvious and subtle. But the problem is not difficult to handle once you see it and understand it.

If your child doesn't like the new addition or wants to "send it back," be suspicious. Watch for sneaky behavior. Your child may avow undying love for the puppy and then pinch it or drop it "accidentally" when no one seems to be looking. So look! If every time you pick up the puppy to cuddle it, there's a little somebody tugging at your arm or thirsty for a drink, you'll have to take some positive action. Give away the puppy? Nonsense! Reassure your child, silly as you may feel, that you love him still, that you love him forever, that you love him *best*. Just as you would think to lavish a little extra attention on your firstborn to help soften the blow of the arrival of your second child, do the same when the puppy arrives. Play with your child a little extra. When jealousy crops up, ignore the puppy, at least when your child is looking. Let him overhear you bragging about *him* a little before you tell your sister that Little Caesar got housebroken in only two days. That way any child can feel free to love a new puppy without feeling threatened.

With a small amount of training, kids and dogs can live in wonderful harmony, respecting each other, teaching each other, giving each other courage, confidence and love. A dog will happily accept all kinds of strange attention from kids. I've never met a dog yet who didn't like to hear a good story, sit in on a game of Monopoly or hear a pleasant song, even a little out of tune. They are super company on long walks to anywhere and almost never tire of retrieving a ball, fetching a stick, racing and following along on a bicycle trip. They are, in fact, tireless companions, while most parents are not. For an active, busy parent, a dog can now and then serve as an affable and willing stand-in. With any luck, he and your offspring will not transmit bad habits back and forth. Your dog will probably never leave his clothes all over the house and your child won't shed all over your couch. But they will enjoy a special rapport, saved exclusively for each other, and possibly keep each other in better balance and better spirits than either would have alone. And while I cannot vouch for a dog's proclivity for nostalgia, certainly your child will remember, long into adulthood, as you and I do even today, the sweetness and the fun of his childhood dogs.

THE MID-LIFE CRISIS IN DOGS

Lately, an awful lot of attention has been focused on that time in life when people feel a paucity of answers and a plethora of questions, a time when old values fail and new ones are slow in coming, a time when goals are modified and discontent reigns, a time of great stress. It has been called the mid-life crisis, and crisis is indeed the word for it.

Dogs don't discover, when they hit middle age, that their lives are finite. Nor do they try to live up to patterns unrealistically set for them in childhood. Bitches don't tend to fall apart and feel worthless when their children leave home. However, many dogs do suffer from deep depression at some point in their lives, a phenomenon not entirely unrelated to the mid-life crisis in humans.

Groomed for a Career

Consider the show dog, literally and figuratively groomed for a career in the spotlight from the time of his birth—or even before. Great hopes and great attention center on the little creature and from as early as he can recall (if dogs *can* recall) he is earmarked for his special career. He is handled, if not more frequently, at least with more awe. Energy, eyes and conversation are focused on him. When he can barely walk, he learns to stand on the grooming table. He wears a special leash, a show lead. He is fussed over, clipped, brushed, coiffed, groomed, bathed, stacked and gaited.

While still a youngster, he begins to travel to Match Shows and there he becomes the attraction for crowds of people. There his life as an applause junkie begins. He is tuned to a higher pitch of excitement than the average dog, marching to the beat of a very special drum. In no time at all, he thinks and feels like a star.

If things proceed as planned, he is bedecked with ribbons, steps up his travel, falls into the capable hands of an excellent handler and groomer and is primped and polished even more than before. He faces larger, more excited, more important crowds. He responds to louder and more intense applause, cheers and hoots. He is photographed, loved, trained, practiced, paraded. He eats the best diet possible. He gets sufficient exercise to keep him in optimum shape. He is, indeed, on top of the world.

Eventually, career dreams are satisfied and travel time slows to a crawl. He may now live with his handler and not his owner. He is more than likely retired from the ring and available by appointment only to approved bitches. To an outsider, his new career sounds like heaven on earth. But that is all just so much projecting. The sex life of a dog is a far cry from the sex life of humans. Being a stud dog is not *something to do*. The dog, during the mating procedure, is driven not by desire and passion but by scent and hormones. He reacts almost totally automatically, as if he were in a semi-trance. He does not spend leisurely evenings at small corner tables in candle-lit restaurants. He does not hold paws in the movies and stroll home dizzy with anticipation. His work is swift. He needs time to retrench his forces in between matings. He needs more in his life than a jug of wine, a loaf of bread and a bitch in season. A hard-working stud dog needs some fun in his life!

Your champion, now retired, may have been a brood bitch. Still, that only took up a few months of her time in the last few years. Now, with two or three litters doing her proud in show rings all around the country, she may just be twiddling her thumbs in the kennel. Even the dog who was worked daily and carefully for his obedience degree may get bored and depressed when his turn to travel is over. What a relief for you to end those seemingly endless practice sessions, seeking the perfect straight sit as the surfer seeks the perfect wave. Haven't *you* earned a rest? Your dog, though, has been led to expect a higher level of activity and, while it is sad for any dog to have nothing to do, it is harder on career dogs when retirement comes.

This situation is more common than you think. By and by, the once-cheered champion ages. As younger dogs rise to take their place in the sun, his activity is more and more limited. Who has time? So while he still eats well and is well taken care of, most of the thrill is gone. No more bright lights, no more clicking cameras, no more dogs and judges to strut in front of, no more applause. Enter the mid-life crisis in dogs.

Accustomed to the activity, enjoying shining health and having the stamina to withstand the joys and rigors of show life, he is suddenly unemployed, out of the spotlight and bored. What can compare to the life he led for years, a life he was groomed for and hooked on? What will he do with all that fabulous energy, all that talent, all that intelligence? Poor little rich dog. Often deep depression sets in. Depressed dogs tend not to eat and drink normally and thus become more susceptible to illness.

The Gold Watch Syndrome

Symptoms may include loss of coat, endless licking at paws, high-strung behavior, random whining. He may get more and more pushy for some attention or he may just seem to give up and lie about looking listless. Here he is, the personality kid. He didn't get to the top on nothing. Despite the fact that his proud owners *do* love him, often they don't *do* anything with him, although he is, when you think about it, material for an ideal pet. He has the good looks, confidence, stamina and health to charm any audience, including the friends you have in for dinner, the people who live down the road, the guy who owns your local hardware store. Even though he's probably not obedience-trained, he has had training for the ring which has taught him to listen and heed. Further training, to make him a better pet dog, would be simple with the grounding he already has, even if he's five or six years old. Of course you can teach an old dog new tricks. Your retired dog, be he four or fourteen, can still enjoy learning new things. Education is one of the best antidotes for the mid-life crisis in dogs. In fact, I hear that getting inactive brains back to work, presenting new challenges and keeping the pace of life exciting even works with people.

Fun and Games To Combat
the Middle-aged Blahs

You have spoken to him for years—in the ring, on the grooming table, in the kennel, in the kitchen, on trips, on walks—so he knows how to distinguish words. If you are now very busy and can't spare much time, let him join you while you prepare dinner. You're getting your work done anyway. He will enjoy the contact and the wonderful kitchen odors. Now, you can begin a game while you work. Take the pieces of vegetable you would discard—the ends of carrots, celery tops, pea pods—and, one at a time, hold them up to your dog. Tell him SMELL IT and watch his nose. When it moves, praise him. If his mouth moves instead, just tell him NO. He's not an unruly puppy. He won't argue back. So far, he's already in heaven. He's being encouraged to exercise his fabulous sense of smell. At the same time, you haven't lost a minute from your busy schedule.

After a few days of vegetable sniffing, take a piece of one he likes (a carrot?), tell him SMELL IT, place it where he can see it and tell him FIND IT. Now he's already working and getting a triple reward while he learns something new. He has a sense of accomplishment, praise from you and a crunchy piece of carrot. This simple game can be parlayed into more and more fun as your dog gets hooked on working while you cook. Some dogs get so good at it that they bring you things to hide so that they can play. Eventually, you can spend fifteen seconds hiding your dog's toy, without letting him peek, and he'll spend fifteen minutes searching for it—and having a terrific time.

Tricks and games are not the only cures for the canine blahs. Any way your dog can fit into your own lifestyle will help him through his mid-life crisis. He can become your shadow, a grand, flashy, happy companion who can join you on long walks, accompany you to shops, entertain your dinner guests. After a short career dogging your footsteps, everyone will know his name and fabulous face so he'll have a purpose, too, in the post office, the stationery store, at the florist shop. He'll adore his new public every bit as much as his old fans. The last thing he needs, after shining in the spotlight, is to get a gold watch and a farewell party, a retirement of isolation, peace and quiet. Luckily, it takes more understanding than time to ward off the mid-life crisis in dogs.

A Remembrance of Things Past

His life, before, was filled with rituals. Moments of excitement in the ring were preceded by hours on the grooming table, so that even now the grooming fills him with anticipation and makes his blood rush. You can juggle around the old routine and make new rituals fill him with joy. Groom him a little, on the grooming table, before an outing. Use his show lead. Gait him down to the mailbox. Let him in on your ritual of drinks at five. His "drink" can be a dog biscuit. He'll look forward to that time as much as you do. Getting included instead of left out is a great way to chase his blues.

But what if you own a major kennel and you have not one but eleven or twenty-seven retired show dogs. Dog shows didn't happen every day. His new excitement can come in spurts, too. Many of the games can be played by several dogs at once for even more fun. Of course, being diplomatic, you'll make sure that every dog playing gets a chance to win, even if you have to cheat. Most cars have room for a few canine pals. So when I take my dog to go for the mail, you can take three. They can come into the kitchen in shifts, play with each other, vie and compete like old troupers in games. You can bring back sweet memories to them from their colorful pasts by clapping and cheering for a good retrieve, a pleasant walk, a good round of FIND IT. Applause can perk up the spirits of any middle-aged champ.

While it's difficult indeed these days to find enough time for all that needs doing, sometimes a pause to give pleasure to a very special older dog can be the best part of *your* day, too. Returning a small part of the joy a great dog gave you and all his fans can be as easy as it is rewarding. And it's a lot more fun than cleaning the kennel.

Getting Through Together

Any change in your life is likely to have an effect on your dog. If you are moving, changing jobs, changing work hours, having a baby, sending a teenager off to college, getting married or divorced or going through any other trauma, your dog will not only notice the physical changes, but he will be subject to the emotional ups and downs you are going through as well. He is particularly subject to sponging up your stress, as well as suffering his own when your life changes dramatically or his does. This only gets magnified when tension causes you to neglect him in any way or to break the patterns he is used to.

Of course, if you feel too harassed or too nervous to cope with his headaches as well as your own, troubles can be compounded. Feeling tense, neglected and confused, he may become ill, become destructive or appear to be spiteful. When things change suddenly, in your life or his, he can be subject to severe anxiety attacks. He feels insecure. He feels rotten and scared. If those feelings make you eat more or drink more or smoke more, they might make your dog use his mouth to discharge anxieties, too. He may use it on your twelve-hundred-dollar couch, even if he's never tasted it before. He may take to hiking his leg on your piano, hiding under your bed, hanging onto you like a second skin. Before you decide he's turned mean or mad, analyze the situation and see what you can do to alleviate his worries.

Five minutes of attention before you leave the house can work wonders for a dog. A long walk, a run, a brief training session, a game of find-the-ball or a soothing five-minute brushing can make him feel part of your life and allow him to relax when you're out. Busy as you are with all your problems, you'll probably feel better, too, if you take time out from biting your nails to play with your dog. If you didn't enjoy contact with him, you probably wouldn't have him in the first place, so taking the time to soothe him may help you relax, too. Besides, coming home to find the house in the same condition as when you left will make the whole day easier to take. In this case, no surprise is the best surprise of all.

It is best to remember, when going through heavy transitions, that, like us, dogs are creatures of habit, are highly emotional and are subject to insecurities and mood swings. Being pack animals, unlike us, they tend to feel more secure in small spaces. A brief period of confinement can help a dog tough out a difficult change. Make sure he has something to gnaw. Familiarize him with the new territory or the new arrival or the new routine in gradual doses and with lots of praise. Try to hang on to whatever you can that's familiar to him and therefore gives him comfort—his walking and eating schedule, the same brand of food, his bed or mat, his favorite toys. Above all, be sure he retains a sense that, in spite of all the confusion, you love him still.

Happily, the investment of a small amount of time and concern will pay you back richly. In times of trouble, the friendship of your dog can help *you* muddle through. You'll feel needed. You'll have company when it's important. You'll feel loved when the pressure is on and you need it most. You and your dog can get through anything when you do it together.

11

Multiple Dogs—
Multiple Problems

There is more light than can be seen through the window.
—Russian proverb

Yes, Virginia, if you have more than one dog your problems will be more numerous and more complicated. But, no, this is not a plea for you to reduce the size of your pack. A little ingenuity and some uncommon sense can see you through. If you have a lot of dogs and a lot of energy, you can even housebreak and obedience-train the whole pack. As with feeding and grooming more dogs, it simply takes more time to train more dogs.

Many people buy two puppies at a time so that they can have twice as much fun and the puppies will always have company. They soon discover that they will have much more than twice as much fun and that it is not good for a puppy to always have company. A puppy must learn to stay alone, to go out alone, to work and eat alone, to sleep alone and even to play alone. If he is with a friend or littermate all the time, he will never have a sense of himself as a separate, independent creature. If this togetherness goes on for a long period of time, any separation could cause one or both of the puppies great distress and even illness. Such strong dependency is a poor idea and will not permit proper training or a healthy upbringing for the dogs.

In order for puppies raised together to feel friendly, but independent, the careful owner must separate the dogs in a variety of ways so that they end up being able to do anything and everything by themselves as well as together. This step should come prior to any actual training. Beginning with housebreaking, if puppies are separated when left alone, you will know who is doing what and when. If not, and you come home to a puddle, you'll have no way of knowing which puppy had the accident, no way of accurately modifying the schedule of the right puppy to rectify accidents and get the chore of housebreaking over with. Left together, of course, the puppies will play. The activity will make them both need to relieve themselves in a much shorter time and, if one puppy urinates, it is much more likely that the other will also in response to the triggering scent.

If you have kennel facilities, a large run or an outdoor pen, puppies can be more easily left together to play. But they are not getting housebroken in this case. The longer you wait to do that, the more difficult the job becomes.

There are other reasons not to leave puppies together all the time as they grow. Since they should learn to sleep alone and play alone, it is just as well to get the housebreaking accomplished at that time. Once left for later, it usually gets skipped altogether. The crate method and schedule described in Chapter 3 is the best method for training puppies, whether you have one to train or ten. The puppies will rest and stay clean, each in a separate small crate. During outings and at play times, the puppies can interact, romp, tumble, mock-fight and exhaust each other. Using this method, housebreaking will be accomplished in a short time, after which you may want to house the puppies together most, but not all, of the time.

Keeping two or more puppies of the same age together all the time also means that a strong pecking order will be established while the pups are still very young. This doesn't give the more submissive puppy much of a chance to feel his oats and may make him overly submissive. The dominant puppy, on the other hand, if he can, will assert himself frequently by beating up the submissive puppy. He may get to feel invincible. This may not be a realistic appraisal of his true position as an object of your training and as a dog in the real world. The alpha pup may end up difficult to train because he's

gotten used to coming on so strong. The other puppy, while a perfectly fine dog, may end up nervous and shy. At the age the puppies
are separated from the litter, they need more time to relate to people, to begin to learn manners, rules and words. They need to be
socialized to the larger world outside the kennel, pen or kitchen.
This is a poor age to keep them together around the clock. Doing so
may make them feel very anxious whenever they are separated.

Ideally, the puppies should experience a wide variety of things separately and together. This is a big commitment. It is even a larger
commitment when you are dealing with more than two puppies.
However, when the pack starts getting tremendous, there are often
more hands around to deal with the dogs. One way or another,
things should be done in the best interest of the dogs, no matter
how many there are.

Add a Method to Your Madhouse

Although there is something wonderful about living in a dog pack,
it takes more planning than living with a single dog. First, each of
your dogs must respond to at least two names. Each must know his
own call name. If you wish to add affectionate nicknames, that is
fine. Second, each dog must learn to answer to DOGS. There's no
way that you can take a group of dogs out safely to park, woods,
field or lake if, when it's time to go home, you have to shout
SHIRLEY, MAX, PLAYBOY, JENNY, LENNY, PENNY,
SADIE, MIMI, SPOT, BARTHOLOMEW, COME! DOGS,
COME is more practical.

Next, you'll need a commitment to housebreak the puppies by
separating them. Once that is accomplished and the puppies have
learned their names, you will be ready to teach them each the basic
commands. The more dogs underfoot, the more necessary it is for
you to have a language with the dogs, for them to know how to listen and concentrate and for you to have the ability to easily and
simply stop all activity when it gets out of hand, as it will from time
to time. Unless you plan to keep dogs kenneled always, they need
training if you and they are to have any sanity.

If you can get help from family or kennel assistants, grab it. Each
dog must work alone on each command, for twenty or thirty minutes. Then each must try his new skill with his canine buddies
around. Work it is. But a multiple SIT, STAY is as cute as any trick

and more useful than you may now guess. If there are two puppies, the job is not too overwhelming. Each puppy can go out for a training session. The puppy left home is working, too. He is learning to stay alone quietly and amuse himself without eating your walls or furniture. Both dogs are benefiting from the whole lesson. After each dog learns to sit and stay separately, the dogs should be put on a SIT, STAY side by side, a few feet apart. Unless you are a very experienced hand at obedience work, you will need a second handler for this part of the lesson.

When the pack boasts two or more dogs, teaching the basics is extremely important. All the dogs should be able to heel, sit and stay, lie down and stay, and come when called. Socializing the dogs well and allowing them to be individuals is more difficult when they are not trained. These tasks will utilize the basic commands. Other problems, which may increase as the dog population increases, are best handled through training and the discipline and language it offers.

Once the dogs have the four basics down, which should take four to six weeks (a command a week, more or less), you should go back to the SIT, STAY and work on perfecting it. The method of doing so, as follows, should be used with each dog individually and then expected of them together. Eventually, you should be able to say DOWN in a normal voice and have eight dogs lie down right where they are, on your kitchen floor or out in the yard. From this initial aim for perfection, beginning with the SIT, STAY and spreading out to the other basic commands, you will eventually be able to say things like ALL DOGS INSIDE, ALL DOGS TO THE CAR and ALL DOGS DOWN. It's nice when you are preparing food, yours or theirs, when company comes or when you need control for safety, to be able to verbally monitor a crew too large to handle on leashes and too large to be able to float around indoors or out without some good basic training.

Perfecting the Sit, Stay

A *perfect* SIT, STAY means that in an unpredictable, real-life situation, the dog will remain put until you give him the signal to break. It means that off leash, outside, on a crowded street, in front of a parading cat, in the presence of your other playing dogs or with someone he loves approaching, the dog will not break. It means that a West Highland White Terrier will not break to chase a squirrel. It means that a Golden Retriever will sit still at the edge of a duck-filled pond. It means that a male Chow Chow will let another dog pass and not break. It means that a Puli will not break command every time a herd of sheep passes by. A perfect SIT, STAY, moreover, can be the key to a perfectly well-trained dog.

It's the Battle, Not the Issue, That Counts

It doesn't matter where you make your stand. It only matters that you make it and that you win. Perfecting the SIT, STAY is important in that perfecting any one command will reinforce your alpha dog position and will do so in a clear and humane way. The SIT, STAY is ideal grist for the perfection mill in that it is easy to teach as well as easy to test and improve upon.

Perfect heeling is infinitely more difficult to achieve, since both trainer and dog are moving and constantly making subtle changes in position and in relationship to each other. It may take a much more practiced eye than the individual owner's to ascertain when the dog is cheating a little, perhaps by just an inch, and winning the endless battle for the top dog position. Doing what you ask, but doing it *his* way, means, in the dog's eyes, that he has won the skirmish.

The DOWN, STAY, another very important command, is not best for this initial honing of training because it is so much more difficult to get a dog to lie down outdoors with distractions around when he is still at an imperfect level of training. While a SIT can be assisted in a relatively graceful manner, without offending the dog, the neighbors or passersby and without falling on your rump, that is not always true of the DOWN. Many of the manipulations and corrections you might have to go through to get your way would offend those watching who knew nothing about dog training and also might cause you to lose your balance. It's best to deal with this tougher problem and to deal with balancing while you step on the leash or bend forward to pull your dog's legs forward after you've made your points with the SIT, STAY.

I have seen time and time again, after an hour-long battle with a single command, that all the rest of the training sharpens. The dog truly understands, when he cannot break to chase a passing cat, that your word is a bond. It is, in fact, as powerful as a leash, even when he is not wearing one.

Most people, especially those not training for the obedience ring, are so delighted when their dog obeys a command that they never even think about getting fussy. The list of excuses they write for the dog is endless. "He's just a dog. He's tired. A car passed by. The sidewalk is cold. I think he needs to go." You may have your own. But once you see clearly how much additional mileage you can get from winning the battle in this not so arbitrary area, you will never look at obedience work the same way again.

Perfection Is Not in the Eye of the Beholder

Perfect is perfect. Certainly, the dog is not a machine. He is alive, mysterious, unpredictable, distractable, silly, humorous, tricky and smart. He cannot heel perfectly—not forever, anyway—but a perfect SIT, STAY means a *reliable* SIT, STAY. That he can do. That he should do. He should understand that your word is his command, no matter what! Once he does, he will begin to trust you implicitly. When he fails to, he gets corrected. You never quit until you get your way—until he gets it right. Eventually, he learns that obedience means no corrections, no negative consequences, a feeling of pride and lots of praise—so why shouldn't he just relax and trust your word. Doing so has its rewards. It begins to feel pretty good to be an obedient dog.

Once your dog has reached this level of perfection, several changes can be noted. First, his attentiveness and obedience will spill over onto other commands. Second, he will stop thinking over your commands, so strong is the point you've gotten across. That means that when there is a potential accident, such as the dog running in front of a car, your quick command *can* save his life. He will not continue to run while he decides whether or not to obey you this time. He knows you'll win. He knows you'll catch him and correct him if he disobeys. He knows you'll praise him warmly when he obeys. You have proven all of that. He does not know that his life is in danger, but you do—and that's enough. That's just one reason why you're the master and he isn't. That's also why you should perfect his obedience.

The third benefit from *perfect* training is that when you most need your dog to obey, he will. He'll not only do it instantly, as in a possible life-threatening situation, but he'll do it when most dogs will not—in the face of the very distractions you'll use to bring him to this higher level of obedience. Most owners find that their dogs may be perfect in the ring, in the yard, in obedience class or in the living room. But when real life crashes in on them, they may find themselves, arms full of groceries, with a disobedient dog. At the most inconvenient time, and this is not a coincidence, your dog may decide to disobey. You can cut down on the frequency of his poor judgment by perfecting his SIT, STAY.

Test As You Teach

You're familiar with the way a dog tests to shuffle around his place in your people pack, aren't you? Well, you can learn from him and work in a similar way. The amount of feedback your dog can get from small disobediences, from his mini quizzes, is amazing. It lets him know if he should move into the presidential suite or stay quietly in the doghouse. Now you can become as adept at testing as he is.

Let's start from scratch, just in case. You may use a flat leather collar or a simple slip collar. Use a six-foot-long leather leash. Leather provides the best traction with the least wear and tear on your hands. Say SIT. If the dog sits, praise him. If he doesn't, pull gently up on the leash as you push down on his rump. *Voilà!* A sitting dog. *Voilà!* He's up. Tell him SIT. If he doesn't sit, make him sit. Move a flat, open hand, palm facing your dog, toward his face, saying STAAAY. Back away to the end of the leash and wait. If he breaks, immediately say NO. Go to him, or to where he was. *Using the leash and not your hands,* place him back in the same spot, facing in the same direction, tell him STAY and depart, as before. This, more or less, is the simple procedure that, with a few frills here and there, will take your dog to another, better level of training and to a reliable, useful, startlingly classy level of SIT, STAY.

Work on the SIT, STAY, varying the time you require the dog to stay, for at least two weeks. Do not do any of the following things:

1. Do not hit the dog.
2. Do not forget to praise the dog after you release him from command. OK is a fine release word.
3. Do not say OK because you see the dog is about to break.
4. Do not quit if you are having trouble. Get it right; then quit.
5. Don't think your dog is too dumb to improve. That ploy may be part of the way *he* controls *you.*

Be sure to do these things:

1. Plan the time of the STAY, by the clock, in advance.
2. Plan to arrive at a half-hour SIT, STAY by the end of the second week of training. Yes, he can.
3. Work in a variety of places. Work indoors and out. Work off your property. When he's good, work him in front of your other dogs and other people's dogs, too.

As the dog improves, his confidence as a worker and yours as a trainer will both start soaring. Bravo. That's all part of what we are after. Of course, you can and should intersperse all kinds of other training with the SIT, STAY. But always concentrate on getting a reliable STAY by using whatever makes the dog break. As he gets better, make sure that you begin to go where the heaviest distractions are. Don't avoid the neighborhood tomcat. When he's out looking for mice, look for him. When you spot him and your dog spots him, put your dog on a SIT, STAY. If he breaks three times, correct him three times. Do not get angry. When your dog gets corrected, he learns, so corrections are a very fruitful use of your energy.

Corrections May Get Firmer
As Your Dog Gets More Perfect

Saintly patience is required when you begin training, but as the dog gets better and as you clearly see that he knows what is expected and how to do that, you may want to get firmer in your corrections when he does slip up. This is particularly true if you are in the position of correcting the dog many times in a row. That usually means that the correction is too mild and that he couldn't care less if you did it all day long. When this is the case, drag him back to where he was sitting without uttering a word. The silent treatment, at this point, can be louder than shouting. Often, now, one good, firm correction, stronger than he is used to, will put a stop to his breaking, at least for the rest of that day's training. As time goes by, more and more of your hard work will carry over to ensuing sessions and fewer corrections will be needed.

Sometimes harsher corrections, at this level, are kinder to both of you. They can get the job done rather than letting it drag on and on. No matter how many times you have corrected the dog, though, the training session should end with a perfect execution of the command and praise from you. Play with the dog after the training session. Let him know how really pleased you are with his work. Avoid using food for praise, but you can give him a biscuit after the session is over. Praise is one of the key factors for a happy, balanced, well-trained animal. The dog should work with excitement and pleasure —and so, dear reader, should you. The better the results, the more likely that is for both of you, so careful attention to the smallest details is urgent, since it will ensure the very success we are after.

Whether your dog will eventually show off his perfect SIT, STAY during those exciting first moments when company comes, at obedience trials or when you are dishing out chow for him and your other eight dogs doesn't matter. The fact is that when you need him to come through for you, he will be willing and able to do so. In addition, you will have developed a sharper eye for detail, a better sense of the subtleties of your dog's fertile mind and a more accurate, assertive hand for both leash work and praising.

Extending Perfection to Your Whole Pack

You cannot hope to be a true alpha dog and get real obedience from a group of dogs if you don't have that with each individual first. Once each dog will hold his STAY under fire, by himself, you can begin to expect perfection from the dogs when they are together. I cannot emphasize enough how important it is to get quick responses from your commands when you do have more than one dog. The benefits extend far beyond getting the dogs to sit while waiting to get into the car or go out for a run.

Once you have more than one dog, you have a legitimate dog pack. The pack affords more courage to its members than any would have as the only dog in a people pack. The dog who might feel lonely and scared when you go out to work will have the help and encouragement and added energy of a buddy or two. Together, they may be more destructive than one dog would dream of being. If you call COME and one dog takes off, the other is likely to follow suit. You are now sharing the focus: all of the dogs but one have two alpha dogs in their lives—the top *dog* and you. Therefore, it is even more essential that you make it clear to the canines that you and any other human who deals with them is more alpha than the alpha dog. While they may kowtow to him when you are not around, they had best all listen to you when you are.

Testing will be more frequent with the added courage of the pack. Therefore, you will have to win the same foxholes over and over again—but it's not all that grim. Once you do the initial training, reminders come quite easily and all the dogs can be reminded simply and at the same time by being put on a long, long DOWN, STAY while you sip a long, long cool drink, pay your bills or read a book. In fact, you should arbitrarily remind the dogs, just as the top wolf does in the wild, that you are the leader, that you are at the top of the heap every minute of every day. No dog will resent you for asserting your rights. Dogs are orderly creatures and like to know where they stand.

Within your canine pack, there will be a pecking order. Unless there's fighting, I'd let the dogs work that out for themselves. When dogs are trained, there's less of a likelihood of fighting and more of a chance for stopping any possible battles with just a word from you. If any of the dogs are a little trigger happy, you may have to or want to separate them when you are not around. The idea is that they can function well together, can function well apart and are under your control when you are with them. The choices are all yours.

Jealousy among the dogs can be handled fairly easily. Of course, you'll want to cater to the old-timers first. If, after that, the dogs get approximately equal attention, they should manage. If they are the kind to be jealous anyway, training can help you out. Whenever one gets pushy and demanding and you are busy with another, send the pest to GO LIE DOWN until his turn comes to be groomed or trained. Once on command, most dogs no longer feel neglected because they are working and feeling useful.

Aggression Within Your Pack

If you are a pet owner and have dogs that fight, two males from the same litter or two unrelated males or females, you may find that things improve with training. Often this situation is caused by an unknowledgeable choice in the first place. Then you find yourself stuck with two dogs you love who don't love each other. Sometimes males will get along until there is a bitch in the house. Sometimes we cannot tell why dogs or bitches fight. Only they know why. Your best hedge against fighting is obedience training for all of the dogs. But you cannot force one dog to like another. This problem can be tough to solve.

Sometimes dogs fight because they are getting mixed-up signals from you. They may simply not know for sure that you don't want them to. In this case, two handlers should work on correcting the dogs when they show signs of aggression toward each other. The dogs, both on leash, should be brought face to face. At any sign of aggression, the aggressor should be jerked back and told NO in a firm voice. Shouting will only further incite hot tempers. You can be strong and firm without raising your voice. Mutual tolerance and tentative friendly signals should be praised warmly and this work should be done daily for short amounts of time. The dogs cannot be kept together when you are not around. If, finally, they seem better able to tolerate each other, they can be allowed together in your presence with leashes on but dragging. Make sure they have plenty of space in which to try to work things out. If need be, you can grab the leashes and separate the dogs—but understand that holding the leashes will tend to make the dogs more aggressive. Even when you pick up a dropped leash, you may change the tone of that dog from irritable to fighting mad. If you can, work outdoors and have a hose handy. If a real fight breaks out, turning a hose on the pair could save them and you. If all efforts fail and the fighting cannot be stopped, it would be kinder to all concerned to try to place one of the dogs in another home.

Aggression within the pack is another story for the professional breeder. The situation here is usually one in which there are many males and many unspayed females. When the females are in season, and even when not, it is very natural for the male dogs to feel competitive. Of course, the amount of aggressive feelings and the severity of the skirmishes depends in part on the breed you are housing. While obedience training cannot solve all problems such as these, it is one of the factors that sometimes helps.

For the professional, there is no choice but to keep many dogs. However, anyone involved in serious breeding has kennel facilities and knows which dogs like which other dogs. Dogs can be outdoors or inside for play and socialization in shifts, keeping mortal enemies apart and letting good friends work and play together as time permits.

Counteracting Dependency

The most common problem when there are several pet dogs in a family is that the dogs are always together and become increasingly dependent, one upon the other. If they are littermates, they may become equally dependent. If you added a second dog, the first may be well used to functioning alone, but the new puppy may feel lost when the older dog is out.

The solution to this problem doesn't happen naturally but takes thinking and planning. Each dog must experience staying home alone and going out alone. If you do not take these precautions with regularity, either dog could be in trouble if the other had to be away. When you have several dogs, you have to think about dependency and the other problems plural dogs can cause. Doing what comes naturally just won't work. This means that you have to plan to take each dog out in turn and also make sure, if you have more than two, that each dog gets to stay home alone, not always with other dogs. Things we cannot foresee will necessitate that an animal must be separated from his buddies sometimes—he's ill, they're ill, she's in heat, he's being campaigned, the old dog dies and the younger dog has no pack, everyone's hunting except Charlie, etc. The dogs must be prepared for any eventuality, just the way they are prepared and seasoned for working in crowds, for the noise and commotion of the ring, for putting up with your kids' friends.

Juggling dogs around, unless your numbers are astronomical, is not that hard and, like so many other things, gets to be a habit. While it might seem mean, at first, to take everyone swimming and leave the puppy home, any dog seasoned in this way will be much better off in the long run. His mental health ensured, he can be left, in an emergency, at a friend's house without your worrying that he'll have a massive attack of separation anxiety and eat their furniture but not his food. For the lone dog in a human pack as well as for the individual in your dog sub-pack, independence is important. A dog must know from experience that he can survive and thrive both with and without his buddies.

Many Dogs—Much Noise

I don't have to tell you how noisy it is to have a kitchen full of Yorkies or a yard full of Fox Terriers. With some breeds, you'd have a job keeping one dog quiet. When there are two or twenty, the problem can be a killer. One dog will bark when triggered by a car door closing, the doorbell ringing, an intruder on your property. When you have several dogs, they will all become instantly incited when any one of them finds reason or feels the need to give voice. Not only will they all chime in, but they are likely to become competitive about the whole show and see who can keep it up the longest and bark the loudest.

If you have small dogs, you won't have the kind of house that's so quiet you can hear your dogs shedding. Large dogs, too, can be pretty noisy, once someone gets going, but there are a few things you can do to stop the dogs rather than letting them go on and on until *they* tire of all the barking. First, of course, the dogs should have some training. It's unlikely that they'll listen to you at all without knowing a few basic commands. Then you can try a direct assault on the noisemaking, a shortcut method for gaining silence. When the barking starts, tell the dogs GOOD DOGS, right over the din of noise. So much for protection. Then, in a firm voice, loud enough to be heard over the racket, say ENOUGH. Often the interruption of *your* loud voice will stop the dogs, even for a moment. If they quiet down and look at you, praise them immediately and toss them a handful of broken-up dog biscuits. I promised a shortcut, didn't I? The biscuits give a palatable second reward, after your verbal praise, and also keep the dogs quiet for another few minutes. Do not, of course, give the biscuits without quieting the dogs first *and* praising them for having stopped barking.

With future repetitions, if your voice can't hold out, bang your hand on the wall or door and shout ENOUGH. Again, reward with verbal praise and *sometimes* use food. If you use the food every time, your dogs will start to make a racket just to get the biscuits. Keep finding new ways to stop the noise even for a moment and then keep it stopped for long enough so they forget why they were barking.

If the dogs have been trained, tell them GOOD DOGS, ENOUGH, DOWN. Most barking dogs will not continue noisemaking from a prone position. After a couple of minutes, release your pack from the DOWN command. They should be quiet unless whatever triggered the barking is still present.

If the dogs do not respond at all to your commands nor to your bent-knee pleading, begging and crying, come on like the Marines. Take your plant mister, fill it with water and wait for the serenade. Try ENOUGH. If there's no diminution of the noise, shoot the whole crew right in their noisy faces. The water won't harm anyone, but the surprise will quiet them, even if it's only for five seconds.

Take heart. Five seconds is progress. If you continue the corrections, the surprises, the follow-up praise, the occasional food rewards, eventually you will be able to quiet the dogs verbally whenever they start marathon barking. While that might not be the same as having one slothful dog who snores through the night and doesn't awaken until noon, it's quite a lot. Except for those rare occasions when the dogs bark at three in the morning (and if they do, they might just have good reason), it's not the initial barking that's so awful. It's the duration of the ruckus that hurts. If you work at it, though, you can have control over the length of time your dogs will bark.

Outdoor barking is another matter. Outdoors, the stimuli that inspire barking are almost constant. I would be hard pressed to use corrections harsh enough to have an effect when many dogs are barking outside. There's the constant tease of smells on the wind, of other animals moving by, of cars, kids, postmen. There's the salty smell from the ocean or the lush smell of the woods. There's the moon overhead or a bird singing. The world is tugging at your dogs when they are outdoors. The least they can do is bark back in response. Of course, the amount of noise depends in part on the breed you house and their number. But this is after the fact. If the dogs you love are noisy ones, they have sufficient endearing qualities to make up for the din. Chew toys may help. Exercise helps. Training helps. Other than that, if you house a large pack outdoors, occasionally you will be reminded that they are there.

12

Carsickness and Other Car-Related Problems

> When a friend is in trouble, don't annoy him by asking if there is anything you can do. Think up something appropriate and do it.
>
> —E. W. Howe, *Country Town Sayings*

Carsickness—foaming, drooling, retching and/or vomiting—is almost always a product of negative reinforcement and lack of experience. Often, the dog that suffers from carsickness is a young puppy who has trouble keeping his balance in the moving vehicle or is afraid during his first few rides. The victim may be an older dog who never sees the inside of a car except when it's time to go to the vet or the groomer. He may even be unlucky enough to get an additional set of rides to and from the boarding kennel when he is abandoned there during his family's vacations. For these dogs, the car becomes a form of mental and physical torture. It's no wonder they get sick.

Yet the majority of dogs love riding in cars. It is a treat beyond measure, the very thought of which fills the dog with uncontainable ecstasy. Why does this disparity exist?

Some of the dogs who love car rides got to go in cars frequently when they were growing up and, fortunately, all the rides did not

end at the veterinarian's office for shots or surgery. They got used to
the motion. They learned how to balance themselves. Perhaps, they
were less sensitive to begin with and so could ride, even as young
pups, without getting sick. Possibly, by sheer chance, since they did
not react badly to initial car rides, their owners tended to take them
along more frequently, thus ensuring that the problem wouldn't
occur. Most rides ended in pleasant adventures or excursions. The
car became something to look forward to and enjoy.

Why some dogs are more sensitive than others is not really the
issue. Any dog can get used to riding in the car, though some will
take the experience with more equanimity than others. The process
of retraining a carsick dog or training a young puppy to ride easily is
the same.

What you want to do is to get the animal to associate pleasant
things with the car and to slowly dissociate unpleasant things. The
car should become part of the dog's everyday existence. As he becomes able to ride well, it will be easier for you to take him along
when you are traveling, shopping or visiting.

Start from scratch and introduce the dog to the car. Let the dog
sit in the car with you. The motor should be off. The door can even
remain ajar. If the dog seems fearful, just sit in the back seat with
him and pet him for a few minutes. After you have reassured him,
let him leave the car, on leash, and praise him again for his bravery.
That is all you have to do, once a day, for the first few days.

If the dog can barely stand to sit in the car, save his meals for car-
training time. With the engine off, get in the back with your dog
and his dinner. Praise him. Tell him OK and let him eat in the car.
Keeping the engine off will ease his first few experiences as well as
saving energy and unnecessary expense.

Once your dog will eat in the car or spend a few minutes sitting
in the back seat calmly, he should be less reluctant to enter the car.
Now, you can put him in the back, close the door, hop in the front
and start the engine. Praise him. Shut the engine off. Praise him
again and leave the car. Go as gradually as *your* dog needs to implement these changes, taking two weeks for each step with some dogs
and just a few days with others. How fast you can go depends on the
age of your dog, his sensitivity and the severity of his problem.

Once the dog will accept sitting in the car with the motor running for a minute or two, without any signs of carsickness, you can
take him for a spin around the block. Make sure he has not eaten

for many hours. In fact, it would be best if his last meal were the day before. That way, he can get an additional reward for his bravery by getting his meal right after his ride. If, at any time, the dog begins to drool or foam, stop the car, shut the engine off and make sure the dog has plenty of fresh air. Windows should be open enough for good air flow, but not enough for him to jump out. If he seems ill and stopping the car and engine doesn't help, leash him and take him out of the car for a walk.

Safest riding for you and pup means he should be in a crate. Then, too, you could keep the windows wide open because, safely ensconced, he could not fly the coop or leave the car. The protected, secure feeling your dog has in the crate would carry over to his car rides and help speed his recovery, but not every car has room for a dog crate.

Once your dog can motor around the block with no incident, you can increase the duration of his rides. Since the energy crisis is upon us, try to incorporate these small trips with your shortest errands. Then, your dog can get the additional reward of an excursion with you in the middle of the ride—something other than open heart surgery or an unpleasant bath and blow-dry. It is just those short hops to the hardware store or dry cleaner that will get him hooked on the joy of riding in your car.

By slowly increasing his riding time and by praising the dog for entering the car, sitting in the car and leaving the car calmly, plus the addition of all kinds of pleasant excursions at the end of each trip, your dog will begin to look forward to riding in the car and will begin to relax when he does ride. This procedure, plus the additional precaution of having him ride with an empty stomach and sufficient ventilation, should end all but the most stubborn of carsickness problems.

Safety for Dog and Driver

I have seen more than one driver speeding along the road with a dog on his lap. There are enough things to worry about when driving without adding any extras. In a burst of affection, a licking dog can obscure your vision, knock off your glasses, tangle himself in the wheel and definitely make you wish you had a crate. Even having a dog in the front is not a safe practice. Dogs tend to go to the floor of a car when they get hot. The distance between the passenger's side of the floor and the driver's side is minute, especially for a big dog who nearly spans the gap just by being there. I once had the horror of having my dog move to the floor and, in settling in, slip his hind leg under the pedals. It was a frightening moment until I coaxed him back onto the seat. Ever since then, I will not allow a dog to ride in the front of a car.

The safest way for the dog to ride is in his crate. This prevents him from interfering with your driving or getting out of the car through the window. It also keeps him safely contained in case of a car accident. In the crate, he can see what's going on. He can catch all the breezes. He'll stay put until you are ready to leash him and take him with you.

If you can't fit a crate into your car, teaching the dog to ride in the back seat is next best. With a small, simple additional bit of training, in fact, he will be nearly as safe as in a crate in most normal circumstances. He should be taught, from puppyhood on, not to run out of the car—in fact, not to leave it at all without your permission.

Put your dog on leash and tell him GET IN THE CAR. He might as well learn English any chance he gets. Praise him for getting into the back seat. Two sets of hands work better than one for this work, so have a friend assist you. Open the passenger window and hand the leash to your friend. Tell your dog STAY IN THE CAR, open the door and get out of the car, keeping the door ajar. Your dog, in all likelihood, will ignore your warning and begin to leave the car. Then your friend will jerk back hard on the leash so that your surprised dog cannot leave the car and you will say NOOOO, STAY IN THE CAR. Continue to work this way until the dog waits. Now you can tell him OK, grasp the leash and praise your dog for getting out of the car. If he's learned so well that he won't emerge on the release word OK, just repeat it once more as you tug the leash toward you. With very little work, you can teach your dog not to leave the car until you say OK. This will give you a very secure feeling and provide practical and necessary protection for the dog.

If you cannot find a friend to help, you can work alone. It takes more strength, more confidence and more agility—but, so what. Have the leash on the dog when you tell him to stay in the car. As you leave, do anything you must to prevent the dog from escaping by bounding across your lap. Use the leash, your arms, your elbows,

a body block, your voice, your shoulder, both hands, prayer. Tell
him NOOOO, STAY IN THE CAR. Now, emerge. If the dog
again tries to bully and push his way out, at least you are on your
feet. Use the leash, your hands, a swift swing forward of your hip.
Just win. He must not get out of the car until you say OK. Work as
if his life depended on it. It does!

Suppose he does slip by you. All is far from lost. You have the
leash in your hand. Just haul him right back in, saying NOOOO,
STAY IN THE CAR. He'll hate being put back in after his grand
escape even more than he'll hate being blocked from leaving. That
makes this a great correction, one he will not want to experience too
many times.

Work alone or in tandem. Practice until the work is firm and reliable so that the safety of your pet is ensured. Don't forget to praise
him each time he emerges after you say OK.

Car Chasing

Some dogs are so enamored of cars that they jeopardize their lives
chasing them. In a way, this difficult and dangerous problem is an
easy one to solve. Your dog should not be out running around loose
and unattended. If he were properly under control, he wouldn't be
able to play sheepdog and herd cars in the first place. However, just
in case you won't take my advice, or in case he pulls to chase cars
when he is being walked on his leash, here are the methods you can
use to nip this hobby before he gets nipped by a car.

If your dog pulls after cars when he is out for his walk, on leash,
jerk back hard (send him flying but keep control so that he lands
softly and not with a thud) and shout NOOOOOO. This is how
you can communicate with your auto herder. Repeat this every time
he gives into temptation at the sight of a passing vehicle.

You can push your control a step further by requiring your excited
dog to sit and stay when cars pass. If he won't, you know how to
correct him. While you are working and he is learning self-control,
think Serendipity. After the lesson, let him herd a ball around the
yard, chase you in a catch-me game or run alongside, sheepdog style,
while you jog. He's got a drive. Let him use it.

If your dog chases vehicles when he's out loose, he's really a menace to both drivers and himself. Try lurking about, acting preoccupied, after having tied a long, long rope to your dog's collar. When

he begins to chase, step on the rope. This will make him screech to a halt. Now, continuing as above, jerk him back and tell him NOOO quite assertively. You can also set up a trap for your little speed demon. Have two friends drive by, the passenger prepared to make some corrections. When your dog starts chasing the car, your friend can shoot him in the snout with a water gun, having laced the contents with white vinegar to give it a sting.

I have read suggestions for stopping this dangerous habit with dangerous corrections, such as bumping the dog with the car door or dumping a bucket of water on him as he nears the car. My feeling is that trying either of these corrections might endanger or even kill the dog with the car door, cause a car accident or result in a dry dog and a soaking-wet passing pedestrian. My hat goes off to those trainers who are athletically above average and can perform these feats safely. I, for one, wouldn't dare and hope you wouldn't either. Instead, please keep your pet on leash, under control and away from moving traffic.

The Last Word on Cars

Some people think their dogs are car smart. They open the front door and let the dog out, sure he'll avoid all the Mustangs, Pintos, Cougars and other wild beasts running around on the roads. If he does, and for as long as he does, it's a coincidence, it's luck, it's drivers with fast instincts and good brakes. A dog's mind is not equipped to understand motor vehicles. It is equipped, however, even housed in the most cautious, fearful, pussyfooting canine, to totally forget all else but the squirrel or rabbit it is set on chasing. When that happens, the most "car smart" dog in the world may end up never coming home again. Don't let him be yours.

13

Bits and Pieces: Almost Everything Else You Need to Know

You must ask the right questions to get the right answers.
—The Talmud

The Art of Hailing a Cab (and Getting It to Stop) When the Dog With You Weighs Upwards of Seventy Pounds

If you need a cab to take your Maltese, Shih Tzu or Cairn Terrier to the vet, the groomer or the animal portraitist, you really don't have much of a problem. You can use a carrier, you can let your dog ride in a canvas bag or you can tuck your dog under one arm and hail the cab with the other. Most drivers will stop willingly for a customer with a small dog.

If, on the other hand, the dog you need to transport is a Newf, a Bouvier, a Scottish Deerhound or even a pleasant little Collie, you may be on the corner with your arm waving in the air for a long time. There's no magic to getting a cab when you are traveling with a big dog. Luck, naturally, plays a part. So does common sense and a little understanding of the human making a living behind the wheel. Several elements will affect his or her decision.

If your dog is large, he does not have to be a Doberman, a German Shepherd or a Rottweiler to strike fear into the heart of a cabbie. A cabdriver may fear, first of all, that your dog is vicious and will bite him. Next, he fears that any size dog will do something fearful in his cab, something that will prevent him from earning a living while he cleans and deodorizes his vehicle. The bigger the dog, the bigger the potential clean-up problem. When you think about it, if you were a cabbie, you'd leave you standing on the corner, too.

The best antidote for a driver's fear is to show that your dog is perfectly under control. Have the dog on a SIT, STAY at your side. Have him on leash. Try to get him to wear a docile expression on his face. If an iffy driver stops, you can then reassure him that your dog is a seasoned traveler, never gets carsick and doesn't bite.

If no cab will stop for you, stand at the corner and wait for the light to turn red. Then you can try my friend Alison's ploy, a no-nonsense approach to getting a cab with her Doberman. "I'll give you an extra buck to take the dog," she says before the light changes. It often works.

Another friend doesn't make a big deal about presenting any passenger but himself. He steps out into the street, hails a cab, opens the door and then whistles for his dog, who was sitting patiently on the sidewalk. Somewhere between blatant honesty, harmless deception and open bribery, cabs can successfully be hailed.

Renting an Apartment or House With a Dog, Big or Little

Finding an apartment in today's landlord's market is getting increasingly more difficult. When you have a dog, especially if he's larger than the landlord's classic standard (not a breadbox, but a Poodle), it can be close to impossible. Sometimes nothing can be done. The law is with your landlord. He owns the building and is allowed to say who and what can live in it. If it were yours, you'd fight for that privilege, too. After all, he's probably been stuck with chewed moldings and stained floors already, to say the very least. When *your* dog barks all day and gives 11J and 11L migraines, he's likely to get an angry phone call. When *your* dog has an accident in the elevator and you can't figure out how to hold it on 11 long enough to get the clean-up stuff, his staff gets stuck cleaning up and other tenants tend to complain to him. His front bushes may have a shorter life if there are male dogs in the building. Or, if you are trying to rent a house, your dog may gradually and systematically destroy the grounds. Any area where dogs are walked will need more frequent and careful clean-up. What's in it for any landlord if he rents to a tenant with a dog?

Therefore, unless you simply luck out, it is your job to tell the landlord or his agent just what *is* in it for him. You must assure him that your dog will do none of those negative things, will be a plus in the building and that you, aside from all that, are an ideal tenant. This is how it works.

First, you must be able to assure the owner that your dog is trained, does not bark when left alone and is completely and properly housebroken. Then, you can point out that dogs in his building mean dog walkers out during the evening, which means the street his building is on, and therefore his tenants, will be safer. The elevator and halls will be safer. Even the laundry room, if your dog accompanies you there, will be safe from hiding molesters. Now, to add even more points to your side, you can assure him of your own solvency, decency, A-1 credit rating, secure job and quiet lifestyle. Tell him, too, that you don't give loud parties but don't object if your neighbors do. Last, but far from least, point out to him, as I am pointing out to you, that it would do no good to lie since if in fact your dog did bark all day or chomp on the elevator walls, you'd quickly be found out and have to give him up (which you couldn't do because you love him) or move (which you couldn't do because it is so expensive and this is the greatest apartment you have ever seen in your entire life). If all that doesn't work, return to your broker and ask to see another apartment.

How to Get a Dog Up or Down an Escalator

Only once, and I hope it never happens again, was I forced to use an escalator with a dog. At best, it's a poor idea. If there is an elevator or there are stairs, by all means use an alternative. If you are stuck, carry the dog if you can—and even if you can't. You cannot walk him onto or off the escalator. So if he's much too big to carry, lift him onto the moving steps, place him down squarely, telling him STAAAY, GOOD BOY. When you get near the top, lift him quickly before the steps disappear under the floor, taking his toes with them.

How to Ride in an Elevator With a Dog

Silly? Just walk him on, push the button and go. Right? Wrong. Have him on leash and at your side. Teach him to sit in the right corner, as you face into the elevator. Then you stand at his right. This puts him comfortably in the heel position, under control, and does not force anyone in the elevator into standing close enough to your dog to get sniffed or shed on.

If the elevator is very crowded or is already transporting another dog, stay off and wait for the next car if at all possible. Two dogs or many non-dog-lovers in such a small space is not the best of all possible ideas.

Revolving Doors—Getting Your Dog Through

Whenever possible, do not go through a revolving door with your dog unless he is small enough to carry. Usually, there are side doors which have a sign reading PLEASE USE REVOLVING DOORS. Don't. Ignoring the sign when you have a dog with you will anger no one. If the side doors are locked, you must wait for the revolving doors to be empty to avoid injury to your dog. He will need more time than rushing humans take to get through. Stop the doors from rotating. Let him walk into a section with you and, as you rotate the doors very slowly, talk him through. If someone approaches the doors while you and your dog are going through, signal them to wait. Once accustomed to revolving doors, your dog will take them like a trouper and at a much more rapid pace. However, he may never be able to go through as fast as a person and it is always preferable for you and he to use the doors alone.

Motels—Checking in with Fido

A friend of mine, who has asked that his name be omitted from this passage, used to take his noisy Fox Terrier with him on long weekends and not tell the motel keeper that she would be in the room. He has been reprimanded by several angry owners for his sin of omission.

It's unfair to motel owners, to other guests and to other dog owners to sneak your dog into a motel. Many motels do accept dogs. You can call ahead to find out and then make reservations. That is much easier than winging it when it is late and you are tired. The next best solution is to bring along a dog crate. If you explain that you have one and that it prevents the dog from doing damage, what hotel or motel manager would turn you away? Of course, add that the dog is crate trained and will not bark in the crate. As an extra insurance, if the owner is nervous or asks, promise to pay for any damage that might occur. If you travel a lot and enjoy having your dog along, a crate will pay for itself in no time. If the idea appeals to you, but your dog is noisy when left in unfamiliar surroundings, read and use The Noisy Dog, Chapter 8, before checking into a motel with him.

Property-Training the Dog

Many owners love the notion that they can open the door and let their dog roam within the boundaries of their property, relieve itself, exercise itself and return home, unharmed. This *no effort on my part* fantasy has caused many dog stories to have sad endings. The real trouble is that every block sports one property-trained dog, one submissive little package who never goes exploring or who dramatically runs, top speed, to the property line but never, never puts a toenail over it. Humbug!

Property-training goes against your dog's nature, which tells him to wander, explore, stake out a claim and mark it, look for adventure, seek out members of his sex and the other one, hunt, chase and, just in general, live life to the hilt. Asking him to pretend there's a fence when there is none is not fair and what's more, it won't work. If you teach him to stay within the borders of your property, within some imaginary line set by custom—human, not canine—he may, if you work long and hard, respond and seem to know what you want. But one not-so-fine day, he will go over the line. Of course, wolf packs have territories, too, and mark borders to signal others that this is their land, but they do not regard these borders as prison walls, nor do they stay rigidly within the borders of their marked territory. Neither will your dog stay within the borders you define for him. There might be a bitch in heat, a squirrel passing, a kid on a bike, a chasable-looking car, a jogger with tender-looking calves, a person he thinks he knows. He'll go, one day, because the air is crisp and delicious and something wonderful is wafting in on the wind. Or he'll cross your line because he feels energy moving in his powerful body and he just feels like running.

The day he goes, he may hurt someone (that jogger, that squirrel) or he may be hurt (that car—or the next one). Don't fool yourself that your dog is property-trained. Put in a fence (yes, I do know what they cost—I had one), a run or a pen, or walk the dog on a leash. Do not expect miracles, for, in this case, you'll be painfully disappointed.

Administering Medicine

The main considerations in medicating your dog are that a veterinarian has determined the proper medication and the accurate dosage and that your dog gets all of the prescribed dose. He may appear to be the perfect patient, but hold a pill in his cheek for twenty minutes before spitting it out and knocking it under the refrigerator. If medicine is just dumped into his chow, he may not finish the meal. He would, then, not be getting the full dosage of medication. Most dogs will readily swallow a pill if it is wrapped in butter, cheese or chopped beef. Liquids for very fussy dogs can be administered by pouring the medication into a pocket between the dog's cheek and teeth, then hold his mouth closed for a moment. A follow-up treat will help ensure that he's not holding medicine in his cheek for quick disposal later—or you can just make an eyeball check to make sure he swallowed.

Ick! Ticks

There's hardly anything more disgusting than a tick. For easy removal—and it better be swift or you'll have a house full of tick babies—coat the tick with baby oil or Vaseline, wait a minute and then grasp it with a tweezers and pull it out. While the tick has its head in your dog, the oil makes it begin to smother; when the oil is applied, the tick will begin to loosen its hold on your dog. Using oil or Vaseline instead of other tried and true methods prevents setting your dog on fire, scorching his sensitive skin or burning him with harsh chemicals. This method can even be used if the tick is near his eye. Be sure to dispose of the tick permanently and not just let it go. A cement block tied to its legs and a quick toss in the river is best. If there's no river nearby, drop the ticks into an ashtray full of nail polish remover or something else equally harsh and flush them down the toilet when they're dead. There's no such thing as killing a tick too many times.

Fleas: Beating the System

Flea prevention beats an all-out war because when you war on fleas, your dog is the turf over which you battle. Most standard weapons against pests are called pesticides. Translation: poisons. For areas of mild infestation, some people use an addition of brewer's yeast to the dog's daily ration to help prevent fleas. The vitamin B in the yeast apparently has an odor unpleasant to bugs and indetectable to humans. Of course, the vitamin isn't toxic and won't hurt most dogs. If you choose to try it, experiment with small amounts to make sure your own dog will not suffer any odd adverse effects.

If you live near a park or woods or your dog plays with flea-infested dogs, the B alone won't do the trick. If your dog runs in the park once a week, you can just examine him immediately after, by back-brushing his fur with your hand or with a fine-toothed flea comb, available in pet shops. Any fleas you find can be picked off by hand, squashed by rolling them between thumb and forefinger and disposed of before you get home.

Should you see more fleas, bathe the dog with a flea shampoo. This usually does the trick. If the fleas have gotten into your rugs and furniture, you'll have to spray with a pesticide meant for surfaces, not dogs. You'll have to vacuum thoroughly. You'll have to repeat the flea bath and housecleaning once a week until there are no more fleas on the dog or in the premises. Actually, the fleas do not live on the dog. They live in the rug, the couch, the cracks in your floor. They only jump on the dog at mealtime and for inexpensive transportation.

Another method of flea killing, fairly gentle to the dog, is flea powder. It is effective yet less irritating to the dog than sprays, tags and flea collars. Always move from the gentlest method to the harshest, hoping you can stop along the way, battle won. If not (some flea seasons are worse than others), send your dog to a professional groomer to be flea dipped and, while he's out, bomb the house with an aerosol pesticide which you trigger to fill the house with a flea-killing fog. You will have to return once and open the windows and then return later with your dog. It's a lot of poison to spread around and makes prevention all the more appealing and worthwhile.

Nail Cutting: A Foolproof Guide

Cutting your dog's nails shouldn't be a problem, but for many owners it is. Some people think that the dog's nails will wear down when he walks outdoors. This is often true for the back nails, which wear down when the dog pushes off with his hind legs to walk or run. It is rarely so for the front ones. Some people have the vet or groomer do the dog's nails, but most dogs do not see the vet or the groomer often enough for proper nail care. Unless your dog goes to the groomer once a month, you should learn to do his nails yourself.

If your dog's nails are clear, you will be able to see the quick, the pink area made up of blood vessels. Ask a friend to hold a flashlight for you and to aim it at the nail from the side opposite the one you are on. This will make the quick show clearly and you can simply cut beneath it, removing the sharp tip of the dog's nail without making him bleed.

If your dog has black nails, you will not be able to see the quick. For optimum safety, cut the sharp tip of the nail with the dog nail clippers, cutting a piece so small that you'd have trouble finding it on the floor. You will just be shaving off the end of the nail. If you do this once a week until the dog's nails are nice and short, you can then adopt a routine of cutting the dog's nails once a month.

If you goof and your dog's nail bleeds, do not panic. He will not die, nor will you. Just let him rest, or rinse the nail in cold water and then keep the dog still for just a few minutes. Once the bleeding stops, your dog will be good as new. Even the most experienced nail cutter will cause a little bleeding once in a while, often when the quick is nearer the end of one nail than it is in the others. So don't let one accident stop you from caring for your dog's feet. If you don't cut his nails, he'll begin to toe out. Sometimes the nail will even grow around and back into the foot. Proper care takes five minutes a month.

Dogs and Cats—Is a Long-Term Treaty Possible?

You cannot force your adult dog to love an adult cat if he doesn't feel friendly on his own. Usually, if you want a cat and don't have one, the dog will adjust to a young animal better than an older or grown one. Begin with a kitten. Introduce them slowly, minimizing your dog's jealousy by fussing over *him*. Correct any aggressiveness and praise any signs of tolerance, curiosity, tail-wagging, affection, sharing or even apathy. Feed the kitten on the counter so that the dog doesn't eat the cat food and keep the litter box where your dog cannot get to it. A calm attitude on your part can help matters along. Many dogs have satisfying, long-lasting feline friendships.

Keeping Your Dog Calm When Company Comes

Frantic canine behavior just when you can tolerate it least—when company comes—is a common complaint. Yet it is surprisingly easy to avoid and/or stop. There are two good methods. First, if your dog's training is reliable, put your dog on a DOWN, STAY before you let guests in. If this is going on over a period of half an hour, that's fine. Use the leash, if you need it, and let it lie on the floor near the dog, the clip end attached to his collar. If he rises without a release, merely put him back in the same spot and tell him DOWN, STAY again. The leash will remind him that you mean business.

Once guests have entered your house, hung up coats, hugged, kissed and greeted you *and* taken seats, the dog, who by now has gotten somewhat used to their presence, can be released. At this point he should be able to go around calmly and reap his well-earned rewards.

If you have taught him GO TO YOUR PLACE, you have another method for dealing with his excitement over new arrivals. The only catch here is that, if your dog's place is in another room, he will just be isolated. He will not be getting used to all the new energy fields. If his place is elsewhere, you can use an alternate command, GO LIE DOWN, which works in any room. This command will keep the dog from jumping all over your company, but he will be in the room adjusting until he is released for meeting and greeting. This training, which sounds difficult if your dog is wild when people come to visit, is very, very easy. The most important ingredient is owner confidence. Good behavior will follow with very few reminders. Of course, praise should be lavished on the dog when you release him.

Sex-Related Behavior Problems: What To Do, What Not To Do

If your dog embarrasses your friends by sniffing, you can inhibit him with leash and verbal corrections. Use the leash, jerk him back, tell him NO. If he sniffs you, slip your hand under his collar and jerk him away to one side, saying NO. He may try to continue this common canine habit for a long time, but with corrections, he will do it less frequently than if left uncorrected and, sooner or later, you'll be able to stop him with just a NOOOO.

If your dog makes a habit of mounting people, he can and should be stopped. The obedience-trained dog usually will not indulge in this annoying behavior. He has more respect for people and for commands. He is not only less apt to exercise off his excess energy this way, but he will be faster to stop when told NO if he should try. A hard tug on leash or collar, a firm NO and a collar shake if necessary will end this behavior problem. Be consistent. Your dog should not treat humans as sexual objects ever.

Some people find it objectionable when dogs mount each other. Puppies will do this in early sexual play when their eyes are barely open. Males will get on the back ends of other males; female puppies and even adults will assume the male position in play. The natural play of animals, unless they are hurting one another, is best left alone. Mounting may occur more frequently when a dog is not thoroughly exercised, but when done among dogs and in play, it is as harmless as tail chasing or running about. Try not to let it bother you. After all, dogs will be dogs.

How To Stop Dogs From Running Away

We like to think of our dogs lying peacefully, happily asleep by the hearth. Home-loving as he may seem, though, the dog is a wandering animal. Although we have taken it upon ourselves to open bags and cans, his ancestral programming, still pretty much intact, says: *Hungry? Roam and hunt!* By relocating and taking side trips, his wild ancestors kept themselves in rabbit, caribou and mouse, whatever the land had to offer. Even when his belly is full, the dog has a yen to explore, a strong curiosity, energy to burn and a good nose for nearby companionship, male or female. Altering a male or a bitch will not stop wandering or the desire for it. It will just eliminate one reason of many.

Although it is merely an inhibitor and not a total preventative, there's a good, easy command you can teach your dog to slow up his escape-making and prevent him from slipping through your legs when you are coming or going, hardly giving you a chance to say NO, BAD DOG! So if he's out running loose, despite your good intentions, because he slips out now and then, try teaching him not to leave the house without permission.

To begin to teach your dog NO RUNNING OUT, tell him OK whenever he leaves the house, just as you told him OK whenever you gave him something to eat. Praise him as he crosses the threshold after you say OK. Do this for a week. The second week, take him to the door. Make sure he is leashed. Open the door, saying nothing. Do not tell him SIT or STAY. Do not warn him. Just open the door. If he begins to leave, pull back on the leash, telling him NOOOO. If he hesitates, tell him OK and praise him for leaving with you. Now that first week is beginning to make sense to him. Always use the leash. Intersperse a quick OK with some training sessions where you say nothing and correct the dog if he lunges forward. I have found this work to go very quickly, even with untrained dogs.

Now you can begin the next level. Proceed if your coordination is good and your dog has passed the second step well. Drop the leash. Open the door. If your dog lunges forward, step on the leash fast. Make a correction by saying NOOOO and pulling him back indoors. Try again. This time, if you can get out without him, hold the door open from the outside. Do not call him, talk to him or tease him to join you. If he is tantalized by the great outdoors, but waits, pick up the leash, telling him OK once it is in your hand, and praise him for happily joining you outside. Do not continue this work. Walk him now for an added reward for his work.

If you are doing well and your dog is, too, you may try a more difficult but more powerful corrective measure. If you leave and your dog tries to go out without the release command OK, you can clip him *gently* with the door. Once the door makes the correction, your work can be considered pretty reliable. It will indeed slow the dog who loves to escape from the confines of home and make raids through the neighborhood. Sometimes, dogs learn this work well enough so that, in normal circumstances, they will not emerge from the house even if the door is left ajar. However, during the mating season (which can be any time there's a bitch in heat in the neighborhood), your male will tend to forget some of his education. Your female might also enjoy running away and finding a mate. Both should be guarded like Fort Knox during this time, kept on leash, and watched more carefully whenever the door is open. The male should be exercised more than usual.

14

Problems With Other People's Dogs

I love war and responsibility and excitement. Peace is going to be hell on me.

—George S. Patton

Believe it or not, I get quite a few phone calls about dog problems from people who have no dogs. One day, the mother of a toddler called. Her child used to play safely in her fenced yard. Then her neighbors got a male Shepherd. The Shepherd would hike his leg on the chain-link fence. If her boy was playing near the fence, the dog's urine would go through the fence and right onto the child. She had spoken to her neighbors, who were unfriendly and uncooperative. She was desperate by the time she thought of calling a dog trainer. I suggested, since the owners would not cooperate in any way, that she should protect her child by hanging a tarp along the fence. Although it would cost her some money, it would end the problem and keep things as amicable as possible. I also suggested, since she described the neighbors as being so unlikable, that she plant shrubbery along the fence as soon as she could afford to. The tarp would take care of the problem immediately and the shrubs would eventually grow full enough to give her child additional protection and to give her family a bonus of privacy.

You can't solve every problem fairly. The woman had no responsibility for the dog, yet the dog cost her money. She did have a responsibility to her baby, and protecting him quickly was an urgent matter. In this case, calling in the authorities probably would not have helped. I'm not sure that they would have considered the dog's transgression as a clear-cut breach of the law.

If, on the other hand, dog feces had been accumulating in the yard next door, she could have called the Board of Health. They would come to inspect and, upon finding an unsanitary condition, would issue a summons. If the summons did not inspire her neighbors to clean up, the call could be repeated as often as necessary. In this case, local laws could help solve the problem and the woman would be spending no more than the price of her weekly phone calls to the Board of Health. While this would not endear her to her neighbors, that is not the point. The point is to get a problem solved as equitably as possible.

Using the Long Arm of the Law

Often, when one neighbor upsets another, a long-term spite fight ensues. Using the law, when it is on your side, is preferable to noisemaking, beer-bottle throwing or any other petty hostilities adults have lowered themselves to in similar situations.

When people let their dogs roam, they are often breaking the law. The first step is to check the law by calling the local police department or town hall. Often, you will get the runaround, but if you persist, you can find out what is legal and what is not. Do not assume that the laws pertaining to dogs will be the same as in your old town. They vary widely from place to place.

Once you know the law, if there is an offending dog, try to find out who owns it. If you can, call the owner and politely inform him of what his dog is doing that bothers you and that it is against the law. The threat is merely implied. At this stage of the game, I prefer honey to vinegar. An owner may have no idea that his dog is being a pest or worse on his daily outings. He should be given a chance to make amends on his own before you call out the troops. Of course, it doesn't hurt to let him know that the troops are on your side, ready and willing to go the limit.

If the same dog continues to offend, I'd call a second time. This time, I'd begin to make notes and keep a record. Jot down the dates of the calls and the nature of the complaint. You just never know how far you'll have to go to gain peace and quiet or safety for your children.

When you have tried your best to handle things in a civilized manner to no avail, or when safety is threatened, it is no longer appropriate to exercise the self-control of a saint. Now it's time to play hard ball. Call the police, the dog warden, the SPCA, whoever you can get to admit jurisdiction over the problem. That, in itself, will take some doing. Even the authorities may try to pass the buck. Laws about dogs roaming free or digging up your lawn or overturning garbage cans are not enforced very seriously or very well. Authorities tend to treat these matters more lightly than robberies, muggings and murders. But if you persist, someone *will* come to your aid. Eventually, they *will* contact the offending dog's owner and, if they do it often enough, he may begin to change his ways.

You can also, if you like, pester back and hope *that* will work. Every time Fido shows up to loot and maraud, call his owner, even if it's in the middle of the night. As long as you stay on this side of the law, almost anything is worth trying.

Some folks, when angered, don't bother to check the law. They just mobilize their forces and proceed. Clients of mine have admitted to returning dog droppings to their rightful owner. Sometimes, when they were frustrated enough, they did it devil-may-care fashion in broad daylight. Naturally, such assertiveness can get the point across. But you no longer have the law behind you when you take matters into your own hands in this fashion.

Touching, correcting or harming anyone else's dog is also a risky business. Besides, the problem really is not even the dog's fault. His misdeeds are the fault of his irresponsible owner. With the exception of using my garden hose or my loud voice, I'd stay clear of acting directly toward the dog, unless my immediate safety or that of my children or my dog was at stake.

Mating Season Blues

If free-roaming males bother your bitch when she is in season, all the phone calls in the world will not help you. Even if you embarrass five or six dog owners into locking up their overzealous males, five or six others will show up the next day. Those dogs, poor, lovesick fools, may be breaking the law by running free, but only you can protect your bitch, by confining her indoors, not out. Walk her on leash and stay close to home. Make sure you wait a full three weeks before confining her outdoors again, and give her a bath before you do. Bitches have been known to attract and accept males even after it appears the heat is over. If you own a bitch, this headache is yours.

Curbing Barking Marathons

Noisy dogs, sometimes tied out early on a Sunday by inconsiderate neighbors, can drive you batty in no time flat. I believe in driving back! If the dog next door woke me early in the morning, I'd call exactly then and complain. I'd do it every time the dog was out barking early or for long periods of time. Almost every neighborhood has one, an all-day howler. It's never the dog's fault. Lots of complaints may embarrass or annoy a rude owner into more responsible behavior.

If the noisy dog next door is in an apartment, you can call or ring the bell and complain. Often, in this case, and sometimes in the one just cited, the owners are not at home when the dog is barking. They may not even know that he barks at all. You can call or slip a note under the door, giving the people a chance to make amends on their own—but don't wait forever. If there's no response and no improvement, a call to the landlord should get some help fast, since this will be a serious complaint in his eyes. Most people will retrain a dog to prevent having to give him up or relocate.

Frequently when people are inconsiderate, they assume that no one will do anything about it. They can let their dog roam and maraud, they can neglect to clean up outside, they can sleep late by putting the dog on a tether and putting a pillow over their own heads. They do not bother to teach the dog not to bark when left alone. They feel confident that no one will bother to complain. Often, they are correct. Most people *are* reluctant to complain even when it is legitimate. They want to be liked. They don't want to be a bother or make a fuss. They don't want to be accused of being unfriendly, pushy or nasty. As a result, rights get eroded, privacy is spoiled, peace and quiet disappear.

Courage, my friend. If there's a dog nearby making your life miserable and an owner who doesn't know it or, worse yet, doesn't care, you still have your rights. You can have quiet, privacy on your property, safety for your children. You shouldn't have to fill in holes

some strange dog dug in your backyard. You shouldn't have to clean
up strewn garbage every morning. If someone is breaking the law
and letting their dog bother you *consistently*, do persist. You can
and will succeed in getting the problem alleviated.

Protecting Your Children

Sometimes persistence is not the answer. Sometimes the solution
must lie with you even when you don't have a dog. This is true
when it comes to the safety of your children. If they are being pes-
tered by a neighbor's dog and you know where the dog lives, you can
and should request that the dog be kept under control—or under
lock and key. But even if there is no particular canine pest at the
moment, your children should be taught how to deal with the possibility of a menacing dog, in case they ever meet one.

As previously stated, children should be discouraged from handling strange dogs, particularly if there is no owner around. In addition to that good advice, they should learn what to do if a strange
dog approaches them and you are not around. Again, they should
not handle the dog, even if it looks friendly. A loose dog may be a
starving stray, may be trigger happy, fearful, nervous, terrified. He is,
at the very least, likely to be unpredictable. Children should also be
taught not to tease dogs—loose ones, tied-up ones, strays, any kind of
dogs. This dangerous and inconsiderate habit is more commonplace
than you may imagine. It is the cause of many a dog bite and sometimes, sadly, this thoughtless behavior persists on into adulthood.

Even when they have not been teased or provoked, some dogs can
take it into their heads to chase running kids. Chasing, after all, is
instinctive in canids. If the dog is just playing at herding, it will stop
when the kids stop. If the kids are chased by a mean dog—a dog
growling, barking, trying to bite—they should scramble up a tree,
make it to the nearest door and get inside or, if they cannot get to
safety, they should freeze. Running and screaming only serve to incite the dog more. Show them once how to protect themselves if
they are cornered or attacked. The best way is to wrap the arms
around the head and bend head toward the stomach. They should
not lie down. A dog is much more likely to bite if you are on the
ground than if you are standing up.

If the dog is a borderline attacker, an assertive NOOO might
chase him off. This depends on the size and ferocity of the dog and

the size and ferocity of your child. You will have to use your judgment with this suggestion. In any case, all these precautions are just that—precautions. It is unlikely that a vicious dog will attack your child, but the child is still better off knowing what to do and what not to do, just in case.

Guerrilla Tactics for Runners and Bicyclers

If the dog from down the block comes and tips over your garbage, you can pester his owner to confine him, you can spray the dog with a cold shower from your hose, you can yell assertively and scare him off, you can secure the garbage in a heavier can with a lid lock or you can booby trap the trash can with balloons. You can even do nothing and just pick up the trash every time it gets dumped. What great harm has been done?

In contrast, if you are out running or bicycling, an uncontrolled dog can be a menace, not just a pest. Now the rule of not harming the dog and of staying within the law may have to be bent a little. Try a simple, nonviolent solution first. But, much as I love dogs, when it comes to him or me—I vote for me!

If you are on a bike, a dog can cause a nasty spill. Riding a bike gives you a great advantage over running, though, because you can carry things without too much inconvenience. When running, carrying anything heavier than a five-dollar bill could be annoying.

If your regular route goes past the house of an aggressive dog, you could change the route. If that easy solution is not possible, you could try calling the owner of the dog to see if he will consider confining the dog. He probably will not. If you are fit and strong, you can try to pedal fast enough to outrace the dog. It is less likely that you could do this if you are on foot. Dogs can be pretty fast.

Try to size up the dog fast. An aggressive dog will have everything pointing toward you—ears, eyes, tail up, hackles raised. A fearful dog will be half and half. He may have his ears forward and he may be barking, but his tail may be tucked under. Don't underestimate him. He is more likely to bite you than the aggressive dog.

The aggressive dog is using power, so he understands and respects it. You might just yell GO HOME and get rid of him. Do not try to make friends with either the aggressive or shy-sharp dog, and do not turn your back on either. Back off slowly while facing the dog.

The sight of your back or backside is enough to make any dog feel courageous enough to bite.

If you are troubled not by an occasional barking dog but by many tough-looking canines, better carry a water gun and lace the water with white vinegar. This is easier if you are riding, but, much as you'll hate to do it while running, carrying a small plastic water gun beats patching up a dog bite.

Some runners and cyclists try kicking aggressive dogs. If you are on a bike, a swift kick could topple *you.* Swinging a leg or anything else at an aggressive dog could be just the ticket to make him even more aggressive and inflamed. It could make him see red and act accordingly. I personally find the idea rather repugnant. I would only consider that kind of physical aggression if I were already involved in a knock-down, drag-out fight for my life. In truth, it rarely comes to that.

In a real emergency, if you are a cyclist, jump off the bike and hold it between you and the dog. If you are a runner, toss a rock near the dog. Do not take your eyes off him as you bend. If possible, climb a tree. In both cases, a scream for help couldn't hurt. If everything fails and you do get bitten, make an all-out effort to find the owner of the dog so that you can avoid painful rabies shots. If the bite is cleaned well with peroxide, you are unlikely to suffer an infection. Most bites do not need stitches, particularly if they are puncture wounds. Ice will help relieve the pain and you can spend the next few weeks getting loads of attention by relating your adventure, embellished as much as you wish. If you do get bitten, you might as well milk the story all you can.

15

Problems of Loss— When You Cannot Keep Your Dog, When Your Dog Dies

There are times when sorrow seems to be the only truth.
—Oscar Wilde, *De Profundis*

Even the most responsible dog owner may someday be faced with the painful problem of having to give up a loved pet. It's no fun to think about, nor to write about. It will be helpful to have a plan, though, if ever you find yourself in that unlucky position.

Before the first feelers go out, make an honest appraisal of the dog you wish to put up for adoption. If he is a young puppy or a relatively young, problem-free, pedigreed dog, your job will not be too difficult. If your dog is a mixed-breed dog, a dog with a behavior problem or an older dog, the job can range from very difficult to impossible. If the dog has a serious problem, such as biting or severe destructiveness, you should not consider putting the dog up for adoption. If you can no longer care for him yourself, euthanasia is the only course of action available.

How To Find a New Home for Your Dog

1. Ask around among your friends, offering an honest description of your dog—breed, sex, age, behavior (good and bad points),

whether altered, any existing medical problems, his training and other skills (watchdog, hunting companion, tricks). Someone who knows the dog may admire him and might be very willing to give him a good second home. Some owners, in order to help secure an affirmative answer, offer a dowry. They may pay for altering, a check up, food for the first year or medical expenses for life. Offer whatever you feel right about. Of course, the dog's own leash, collar, bowls and toys should go along with him to make *him* more comfortable with the change.

2. Prepare an attractive flyer or poster. If possible, include a nice photograph of your dog. The poster can read as follows:

Please Post or Announce:

FREE TO LOVING HOME— SERIOUS INQUIRIES ONLY

Dog's Name: ROCKY
Breed: Puli (Hungarian Sheepdog) AKC registered
Sex: Male   Age: 4 years old   Color: Black
Height: 17″   Weight: 34 lbs.

Rocky has had basic obedience training. He is housebroken, great with kids, OK with our cat, terrific with other dogs. He's gentle but an alert watchdog, is very healthy and is up to date on his shots. AKC papers and medical records supplied.

We are heartbroken to give up our pet, but we must. We'd be happy to meet anyone who thinks Rocky would give them as much pleasure as he has given us. Please call: CI9-6756.

Have the flyer copied or offset-printed, attach a photo to each copy and mail the flyer, with a brief note, to your veterinarian, all other veterinarians in your area, the local kennel club (if the dog is purebred), the closest breed club of your dog's breed, any training schools in the area, any groomers in your area, pet shops, canine food suppliers. In addition, you might be able to get your sign posted in the window or on the bulletin board of the local college or at any business establishment where you are a customer. Animal shelters also keep a reference file. Instead of taking the dog to the shelter, call them and see if they will register him. In that way, if anyone is looking for a dog like yours, the shelter will give them your number and you will deal with them directly. The dog does not have to wait in the shelter until he is adopted. He waits right at home with you.

3. Speak to your vet, the local kennel club, any trainers who will lend you an ear. The personal touch helps. You might hit the right person on the right day. Ask if they can give you any further suggestions for finding your dog a good second home.

4. Place an ad in the local papers, condensing the information in your flyer. Don't be dishonest, but make the dog sound good and display your feelings for him.

5. Take the dog everywhere with you. If he is admired, you can mention that, although it breaks your heart, you have to give him up. You may get some serious interest. Do not, of course, give your dog away on the spot. Invite the person and any other household members to come and see the dog and your family at home one evening so that you can seriously discuss this possibility.

6. Try some long shots. If your dog is gentle, try calling local homes for the elderly, rehabilitation centers, psychiatric hospitals, schools for disturbed or chronically ill children. More and more work is being done with animals as aids to therapy and recovery. A calm, easygoing dog might find a nice, second career working in a hospital or institutional setting. In this case, if you luck out, whether the dog is mixed or purebred will make no difference at all.

7. If none of the above works and you are out of time, you will have to choose among boarding the dog until you find him a suitable home, placing him in the best local animal shelter you can find or having him put to sleep by your veterinarian. Do be aware that the shelters only can take a dog in when they have room and that many have a limited amount of time during which they can keep the dog available for adoption before euthanasia is necessary. The supply of dogs, unfortunately, is greater than the demand.

When Your Dog Dies

Since no one likes to think about death, a dog owner may find that, although he knew his dog was pushing on in years, he never thought about the practical problems the dog's death would cause.

If the dog dies at home, his body must be disposed of in some way. Once this decision is out of the way, you can deal with the important emotional impact his death will have on you and your family.

If you own a house, a quick call to the Board of Health will let you know if it's legal to bury your pet on your property. For many owners, this old-fashioned, inexpensive solution is the most satisfying.

If burial is not legal in your area or you do not own property, you can have the dog cremated by your veterinarian or your local shelter. The fee is usually small. This, too, many feel, is a very decent way to dispose of your pet's remains.

Some owners feel that, to satisfy an emotional need they have, they must have their pet buried at an animal cemetery. This is a very expensive route to take; however, for some, it is the only acceptable one. You can find out where the animal cemeteries are by looking in the Yellow Pages and local newspaper ads. Some owners even prefer to make arrangements in advance and to know that when the time comes, everything will be taken care of with just a phone call.

If none of the above routes suits you, you may be able to arrange with the local rubbish removal company to cart your dog away. While this method sounds excessively cold and unattractive, it will not matter to the dog—nor will it diminish the love you felt for him when he was alive. You must do what feels right to you, not something that will impress or please anyone else.

Once the practical end is taken care of, no one need advise you how to cope with your loss. Some people rush right out and find another dog before the tears dry on their cheeks. That may be exactly what they need to do. Others wait until the edge is off the pain, until they can talk about the good times without falling apart entirely. Then they take their time and find another perfect dog to fill their empty spot. I have also met some who swear, after a painful loss, that they will never do it again. I, for one, would not want to be long without a dog. Follow your own feelings; you will know what's best for you.

16

The Problem-Free Canine

Bygone troubles are good to tell.

—Yiddish proverb

Now that you understand the nature of dogs and have corrected stealing, biting, howling, nipping, pirating teddy bears, jumping up, pulling, begging and urinating indoors, you can relax about the small things, those harmless quirks that make your dog's personality colorful. Now it's time for some final tips for you and your problem-free dog.

TWENTY-FIVE TIPS FOR BETTER DOG TRAINING

1. Start at the top. You won't get anywhere with your dog if you don't get through to his head first. Once he learns how to listen and pay attention, you can teach him anything. The easiest route to teaching the dog how to learn is by teaching him the SIT, STAY and working until he is clear that he must sit and stay *when* you tell him to, *where* you tell him to and *for as long as* you tell him to.

When he begins to watch your face rather than looking around for an escape, he has learned how to learn.

2. Train with his stomach empty (though not painfully so) and yours full (though not painfully so).

3. A good run before and after a training session makes a nice sandwich.

4. Always keep a collar on your dog when you are home. In this way, you can make a professional-feeling correction at the moment he does something wrong. The collar will also be a reminder to him that good behavior doesn't cease to be important when the training session is over.

5. The mildest correction *that works* is the proper one to use.

6. Try to use a great variety of locations for practicing with your dog. He cannot generalize from your yard to the rest of the world. He can generalize from one store to another, from one shopping center to another, from one dog show to another.

7. Expect perfection from your dog and yourself. Then you can be pleased when you are ninety percent there. If your goals are too modest, so will the results be.

8. Don't be afraid to improvise. The methods that work for everyone else's dog might not work for yours. If you find a method that is new and humane and that works, that is good dog training.

9. Vary the time of your training sessions so that your dog doesn't quit after fifteen minutes or a half hour. There should be at least one hour-long session a week.

10. As soon as the dog knows a command, integrate it into your normal everyday life with him. If it is a command you cannot make use of, don't bother to teach it in the first place.

11. Always keep the element of surprise in your training sessions. The brighter the dog, the more important this is. You can break into a game or play session in the middle of working and then go back to training. You can intersperse a silent session in with the regular training. You can use just your voice and no hand signals for a session. You can train in a new, exciting place and let the dog explore for a reward.

12. As your dog is learning to perfect old commands, slowly keep adding new commands and new variations of the old ones to keep him interested.

13. Change the order of the commands and do not work in a set pattern. Do not let the dog predict what you are about to do or he will begin to jump the gun. If and when he does anticipate commands, correct him and immediately change the order of what you are doing.

14. Do not test the dog's training in any way that will break his trust in you. Do not try to fool or trick the dog into breaking so that you can correct him. Normal distractions (people, cats, dogs, kids on bikes, noise, food) will be enough testing for any dog.

15. Unless you have a dog who is a real ham, do not use the training for purposes of showing off to friends and family. Many bright dogs react badly to a silly use of their serious education.

16. Do not let children or childish adults shoot chains of commands at your dog just because they know he's trained and can carry them out. Many dogs have the ability to distinguish between this use of commands and a more useful and serious application of them. They will begin, on their own, to ignore almost anyone but you. Your dog should not be given a command unless he is going to be made to obey it.

17. Avoid the use of food during a training session. When there is food around, a great deal of the dog's concentration is on the food and not on the work at hand. He *will* learn, but his work will have a trick-like quality to it and not get to a more serious level. Also, when he wants to break more than he wants a snack, or when you do not have a treat with you, his work will be less than reliable.

18. When working with a shy or nervous dog, proceed very slowly and praise at the slightest appropriate opportunity.

19. When training two or more puppies at the same time, train each puppy alone and then train the puppies together. Do not wait until the end of the course to put them together for work, but do it for a short period at the end of each practice session. When the puppies work together, each must have its own handler.

20. Have a specific goal for each training session with your dog. While you may well work on several commands during the session, you should plan to concentrate on seeing real improvement in one detail before you end for the day. For example, your dog's heeling may be okay, but he may be very sloppy on the automatic sit. In this case, you can have him heel for only a few steps at a time, stopping frequently and hammering away at a nice, straight sit until you get one without assistance. When you do, praise enthusiastically and immediately move on to another area of training. When your dog has finally done something right after a long struggle, do not go for that one extra time. That takes all the joy out of it for the dog. And if he fails to repeat the sit, you'd have to start all over again. His true reward, when he gives you the sit, is to get on to something else.

21. Keep your concentration on your dog. If you are training him and begin to window-shop at the same time, your dog will feel the loss of concentration and begin to work in a sloppy fashion. Then he will just drift off and stop working altogether. If you wish to window-shop or chat with a friend, do so after releasing the dog from his command. It is much more realistic to do that than to deny yourself these pleasures because you are training your dog. Besides, in this way the dog learns an important lesson—that commands are to be obeyed whenever they are given, not just during an uninterrupted training session once a day.

22. When working with a beginning dog, it is important to work every day. If the weather is forbidding, it is better to work indoors than to skip a day. That is a good opportunity to improve the long DOWN, the SIT, STAY, the COME when called and the STAND, STAY. When your dog is beautifully trained, you will simply be using the commands as part of your routine. However, it is always a good idea to give a formal lesson now and then to polish up the work. More than likely, the dog will not only profit from this refresher course, he'll enjoy it, too.

23. Be consistent. Be kind. Be firm. Be clear. Be cheerful. Work with your tail wagging.

24. Education should never end, for you or your dog. There are many excellent books on obedience training, scent work, retrieving. You can pick up new ideas, and share some that you have, from dog-owning friends, at dog shows and from your vet, your trainer and

your groomer. You can discover a new passion—tracking, field trials, trick training. We have just begun to understand the capacity of a dog's mind. The more the dog learns, the better he learns, the more interesting he becomes, the more you learn about him, and so on. Of course, you can teach an old dog, and an old dog owner, new tricks.

25. Don't forget that your dog is a dog. I am often asked, in a daring manner, why my dog is not heeling or sitting or doing something trained and intelligent at a given moment. A well-trained dog has the capacity and willingness to obey a command when it is given. He is not required to work every minute he is awake. I like to let dogs pull hard on the leash sometimes when they have not been asked to heel. Not only do they enjoy doing this very much, but it is very helpful to me when I am walking uphill. The more serious you are in your training program, the more playful and fanciful you can be with your dog when he is not working. Surely, like us, he needs both sides of the spectrum.

INDEX

Active method, dog training and,
  15–16
Aggression (aggressiveness), canine,
  61–80; biting, 61–71, 73–75, 78–79
  (see also Biting); castration and, 74;
  cats and dogs, 154; and chasing (see
  Chasing); dealing effectively with,
  61–62; growling and, 61–62, 63,
  64–65, 69, 72–73, 76, 79–80;
  multiple dogs and, 127–28, 135–36;
  nipping, 61, 63, 69, 71;
  object-stealing and -guarding, 48–49;
  prevention and correcting, 62–75;
  professional help with, 73; sex and,
  75–76, 77, 136; toward children,
  116–19, 158–60, 162–63; toward
  other dogs (dogfights), 76–77 (see
  also Fighting); toward uniforms,
  77–79
Animal cemeteries, 168
Anxiety, 124–25 (see also Fear;
  Shyness; specific problems); changes
  and, 124–25; multiple dogs and,
  128; spite and, 39–40
Apartment (or house): elevators, 149;
  escalators, 148–49; renting, 147–48;
  revolving doors, 149
Assertiveness training for dog owners,
  14–20 (see also specific problems,
  situations); active method, 15–16;
  and housebreaking, 21–37; observing
  dog's behavior and, 18–20; passive
  method, 15; serendipitous method,
  16–18; and stealing, 38–49

Babies, new, in home, 115–19. See
  also Children
Balloons, scratching and use of, 110
Barking, 93–103; avoiding use of
  shock collar, 99–100; being left
  alone and, 94–95, 97–99; car riding
  and, 101–2; commands and
  controlling, 95–97, 98–103; multiple
  dogs and controlling noise indoors,

137–39; other people's dogs and,
  161–62; for protection, teaching,
  102–3; spoiled, 100–1
Beating. See Hitting
Bed: allowing dog in, 58–60; dog
  under, biting and, 78–79
Begging, 50–51
Bicyclers (or runners): exercising dogs
  and, 9; other people's dogs and,
  163–64
Biting, 61–71, 73–75, 78–79, 80; care
  of bites, 164; dangerous dogs and
  final option clause, 80; dog under
  the bed and, 78–79; fear biter vs.
  aggressive dog, 70–71; goosey dog
  and, 70–71; handling hurt dogs and,
  118; and nipping, 71; other people's
  dogs and, 162–63; preventing and
  correcting, 62–71, 73–75, 78–79;
  professional help with, 73; runners
  and bicyclers and, 163–64; sex and,
  75–76
Bones, growling over food and, 79–80
Brewer's yeast, flea prevention and, 11,
  152

Cab hailing and riding, 146–47
Career dogs, retirement and mid-life
  crisis and, 120–24
Car riding, 101–2, 140–45; car
  chasing, 144–45; noise and, 101–2;
  safety for dog and driver, 142–44,
  145; sickness, 140–42
Castration, aggression problem and, 74
Cats and dogs, 154
Cemeteries, animal, 168
Chasing: cars, 144–45; children,
  162–63; runners and bicyclers,
  163–64; snatching objects and, 79
Chewing destructiveness, 104–11
Chew toys, use of, 105, 106
Children, 115–19; dog's fear of,
  89–90; fear of dogs in, 118; and
  handling dogs, 118, 158–60,